Daughters of de Beauvoir

Simone de Beauvoir

Daughters of
de Beauvoir

Penny Forster and Imogen Sutton, editors

The Women's Press

First published by The Women's Press Ltd 1989
A member of the Namara Group
34 Great Sutton Street, London EC1V 0DX

We are grateful to the following for their kind permission to reprint previously published material:
Jonathan Cape and the Estate of Simone de Beauvoir for extracts from *The Second Sex*.
Andre Deutsch and the Estate of Simone de Beauvoir for extracts from *The Prime of Life*; *Memoirs of a Dutiful Daughter*; *Old Age*; and *A Very Easy Death*.

Except where otherwise stated photographs of Simone de Beauvoir are reproduced by kind permission of Centre Audiovisuel Simone de Beauvoir. Copyright Centre Audiovisuel Simone de Beauvoir.

British Library Cataloguing in Publication Data
Daughters of de Beauvoir.
   1. Society. Role of women.
   Theories of Beauvoir, Simone de, 1908–1986
   I. Forster, Penny   II. Sutton, Imogen
   305.4'2'0924
   ISBN 0-7043-5044-0

The film, *Daughters of de Beauvoir*, is available for hire from
Arts Council Film Sales, 105 Piccadilly, London W1.

Typeset by AKM Associates (UK) Ltd, Southall, London
Printed and bound by BPCC Hazell Books Ltd,
Member of BPCC Ltd, Aylesbury, Bucks, England

To our mothers, Doreen and Heather

Contents

Photographs of Simone de Beauvoir between pages 4 and 5

Acknowledgments

The process of this project coming to fruition was at times frustrating. From inception of the idea to transmission of the programme on television took three years. During this time, we were enormously grateful to those individuals who helped us, picking us up as we flagged, and cheering us on to the finish. Rodney Wilson at the Arts Council and Nigel Williams at the BBC took the project on in the first place; Leslie Megahey at the BBC gave it crucial aid at critical times. Roger Thompson and Heather Mansfield at the BBC gave us much practical help. Mike Dibb gave us great support from the start of the project to the end. Our film crew – Chris Sugden-Smith, Louise Stoner, Stephen Bailey and Flora Gregory – were always encouraging and meticulous, becoming more involved than is usual in their professional commitment. Film Editor Alastair Mitchell and his assistant Tim Hands were pillars of strength, once again giving commitment far over and above the call of duty.

We would especially like to thank Hélène de Beauvoir for her time and trouble in helping us, and her warm kindness; the Estate of Simone de Beauvoir for their help; and the Centre Audiovisuel Simone de Beauvoir for providing much research material.

At the The Women's Press, all of whom have shown us a great deal of kindness and support, we would like to thank most warmly Ros de Lanerolle for her encouragement and commitment; and our editor, Sarah Lefanu, for her unfailingly sympathetic good sense and judgment.

Finally, we would like to pay a small tribute to our own mutual friendship which has sustained us through the pitfalls and triumphs of the last three years; and to our partners Dick and David who, as ever, have been wonderful.

Introduction

I was a teenager when I read *The Second Sex* for the first time; I remember the passages on menstruation most vividly. I was newly inaugurated into the business of blood each month; blood every month – did it really happen to *all* women? I would stare out of the window of the bus and gaze at the women around me. 'So, she is probably bleeding now . . . and her, and her.' It made me identify with other women in a way I had never done before. And *The Second Sex* was not just about me, it was about all women. Women bled, and they had bled . . . centuries upon centuries of women bleeding.

After that Simone de Beauvoir was constantly at my side; she travelled with me on holidays, stuffed into rucksacks; next to my bed, she supported me through university, through grotty jobs, and unresolved relationships. And then Simone de Beauvoir was dead. She was no more. And I couldn't believe it. I still had the books – the well-thumbed passages to turn to, the pleasure of re-reading and always finding something new – but she was not with us anymore. I would never be able to make the film about her that had been nestling in the back of my head for ten years since I had begun work in the film industry. Just when I might have been able to pluck up courage to contact her, and feel capable of directing a film which might go some way to expressing my debt to her – now I could not. It wasn't even a possibility. Or was it?

The day after she died I had to go to the local library to do a pile of mindless photocopying. Standing over the smelly machine I began to think about the film I might have made. How would I have approached it? Who would have been in it? And it was then I realized that the film I wanted to make could still be made. It was not a film about her life-story – after all, she had written many volumes on the subject, no, it was a film about what she meant to me and to many other women around the world who had been similarly influenced by her. Not just by the books, but by her as a symbol in the world; her life, full of paradoxes as it was, spoke to us directly, forcefully, and the details showed another way women could live.

A passage readers often cite as a favourite is her description of walking in the South of France as a young teacher:

> I trudged on foot along copper-coloured cliffs all the way from Cassis to La Ciotat, and was so elated by the experience that when I caught the little green bus back that evening all I wanted to do was start off on the same trip again. The passion which caught hold of me then has persisted for over twenty years, and age alone has extinguished it: during those first twelve months it preserved me from boredom, regret, and several sorts of depression, transforming my exile into a holiday.

from *The Prime of Life*

Why is it so appealing? Why do I constantly re-read it? It is because it describes the joy of independence, of risk, of being oneself in an unknown world, of exploration and health. And yet she also describes her loneliness – away from Paris, from Sartre, her sister, and her friends. She offers a description of the many sides of being a woman, and they are all true.

I always knew I wanted to have children, whereas she knew that she didn't want to be a mother (apart from when she was a young woman with her cousin Jacques). Ironically, it was during pre-production on the film that I became pregnant, and while filming in France my morning sickness was at its worst. So while I worked on a film about her, I was involved in a very different sort of experience to any she had had. And yet I could still find a dialogue between us on the subject. Most women who appear in the film talk about her decision not to have children; some are puzzled, others supported by the knowledge that she made a conscious decision that she did not want to have children. Marge Piercy comments:

> she was very clear about the choice, very clear about the reasons she was making it, very unapologetic about it. It seemed to me a clear and sunny, rational yet felt choice.

And yet here we all were, looking to her for the encouragement and example we might look to our mothers for. As Ann

Oakley says:

> Simone de Beauvoir has been a very important role model
> for me, as she has been for lots of other women, and in that
> sense she has been a mother, the mother some of us perhaps
> wished we had ourselves.

When Penny Forster (the producer) and I knew the film
was to be financed by the BBC and the Arts Council, we began
to look for women who would appear in the film. Some were
obvious choices, if they agreed – her sister Hélène, her adopted
daughter Sylvie le Bon de Beauvoir, her old American friend
Kate Millett. It was a conscious decision not to have biographers
in the film, although we wanted to include writers who had
written eloquent pieces about her, or whom we had heard speak
about her – Marge Piercy, Ann Oakley, Eva Figes and
Margaret Walters. It was clear, though, that we needed to have
voices in the film that were neither famous nor literary. We
began by calling them 'ordinary women' and soon came to
know them as our 'extraordinary women'. The *Guardian*
Women's Page published a short piece describing our search for
women of different ages and backgrounds who had been
influenced by, and even had their lives changed by, Simone de
Beauvoir. The response was fantastic. Letter after letter came
from very different women, describing their lives in relation to
her books and her life. Not all the comments were favourable.
Joyce Goodfellow says of *The Second Sex*, 'The book should carry
a health warning.'

How to choose between them? Eventually we opted for a
wide range of age and experience – the young writer Jenny
Turner in Edinburgh; Marta Zabaleta Hinrichsen, an Argentinian living in Essex as a political refugee; Angie Pegg, whose
experiences as a housewife with small children reflected many
women's lives; and Joyce Goodfellow, who was brought up in
south London before the war and presents a view of *The Second
Sex* that is strikingly different to those of the other contributors.

It is in the nature of documentary film-making that you
begin editing even before you begin filming. You have to choose
your contributors and there is always someone else you wish you
could have fitted in. While filming you can never film
everything you might want to; there is always a quotation or two
you didn't have time for. And when it comes to the post- **3**

production editing, you inevitably end up cutting material that is excellent and thought-provoking – a one-hour film just does not allow enough time to fit it all in. This is why we were so delighted when we were offered the opportunity to do a book based on the film. Here was a chance to include these women's contributions in their entirety. The chapters are all based on my interviews with the women. The questions have been cut so that the voice of each woman is clear and unhampered by the question-and-answer process, but these are the 'voices' of the contributors, not written pieces by them. The quality of intimacy comes from the fact they were originally conversations about a shared enthusiasm. They cover the many aspects of women's lives which Simone de Beauvoir wrote about and conveyed through her 'exemplary' life.

It was interesting that as the filming progressed the film crew (unusually, half men and half women) grew more and more thoughtful. Copies of Simone de Beauvoir's works appeared and were read *en route* to the next location. After Angie Pegg's vivid and moving account of the change in her life as a housewife after reading *The Second Sex*, the cameraman was very quiet. 'She has just said what my wife tries to explain to me. I'll have to talk to her when I get home.'

I believe what Kate Millett says is true:

> This great pioneer, the one who'd led the way, wasn't there any more. Yet at the same time she was now inside all of us to an extent. We'd have to find the way through, consolidating everything that she had already taught us. Now we were going to have to remember it – and become it.

Somehow, Simone de Beauvoir has become a part of us: a heroine, but an equal too.

Imogen Sutton
April 1989

Simone (right) and Hélène with their mother

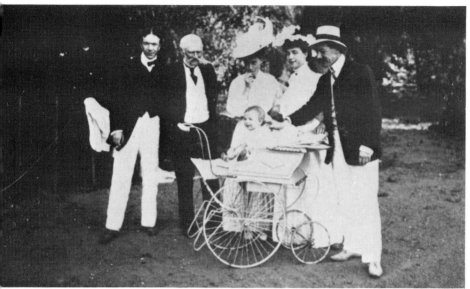

above Simone de Beauvoir as a baby, with her father (far right)
and her mother (next to him)

below Aged 5. Her sister says of this photograph:
'Already you can see she is a little philosopher'

above Aged 18, with Hélène (left) aged 16

below With Hélène and their father on holiday at Meyrignac,
in the Limousin

above (left to right) Simone with Za-Za, her childhood friend, and Hélène

below At the Lycée in Marseilles

Student days at the Ecole
Normale Supérieure, Paris

below With Nelson Algren
in America

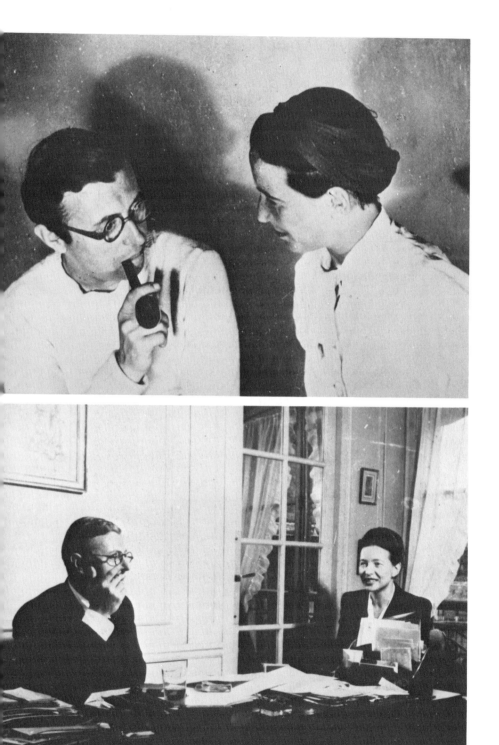

left Simone de Beauvoir and Jean Paul Sartre on holiday in
Juan-les-Pins, and working together in the 1930s

above Simone de Beauvoir in 1947
Photo: Hulton-Deutsch Collection Ltd

above
Simone de Beauvoir with her mother, 1954
Photo: Gisèle Freund, from the John Hillelson Agency

below With Sartre in the 1950s

above
Simone de Beauvoir with Claude Lanzmann meeting Nasser, 1967

below
Distributing *La Cause du Peuple* with Satre

above
With Sylvie le Bon de Beauvoir

above left
Yvette Roudy, Simone de Beauvoir and Kate Millett

below left
With Sartre and Sylvie le Bon de Beauvoir

above
On holiday in Italy, 1981

above left
The funeral of Simone de Beauvoir,
19 April 1986

below left
Hélène at the graveside
(Both pictures courtesy of Hélène de Beauvoir)

Simone in her Paris flat

Hélène de Beauvoir

1
Hélène de Beauvoir

Simone always called me '*Poupette*' [Dolly], and I always called her '*Mone*'. I think I'm the only person who never called her '*Castor*' [Beaver]; she was always '*ma Mone*'. Her friend René Maheu started calling her Castor – he said, 'You have a constructive spirit and you walk in company,' because she always had a lot of friends.

We were very close when we were little girls. My mother was a little anxious because she understood the person I admired most was Simone. I think that is why I became a feminist: I could never imagine that men were better than women, because for me Simone was the most extraordinary person in the world – I always thought that. I still think that.

She did dominate me, but she never oppressed me – that is different. She was like that because she was the eldest and she was strong, she had everything to dominate me. But she was very good with me, very nice, and it was easy to be dominated. I couldn't easily be dominated if people were not nice to me. If you are wicked, I become wicked too.

My parents were very different . . . almost as if they were from different planets. My mother was a real *oie blanche*, you say in English 'white goose', the kind of girl who does not know anything about life, has not tried anything. My father was '*le vrai boulevardier*', a real man of the world, the type of Parisian man you saw before the Great War, men who went to theatres and cafés and went into society. He lived his life and he wanted to marry a virtuous woman to be sure his wife would never have a lover – and my mother never did. He liked an easy life. She was a woman of strong duty, you see, she thought a great deal about duty.

In some ways, I think their differences were good for us, because we had the example of Zaza [Simone's beloved schoolfriend], whose parents were Catholic and both had the same attitudes towards life, and she had no door to enter the outside world. She was smashed by it, and she died. We had a very high education, a very rigid education, and in fact our father, without willing it, showed us the opening of a window – and we went through it.

My mother was always a little afraid of Simone. I think I was closer to her because she was never afraid of me. When I was a little girl I adored my mother but later I had a very difficult relationship with her because when I began to have a little personality she didn't like it, she always wanted to treat me like a little girl. I was to be more like a little girl than Simone. I didn't go along with it, and so I had a bad relationship. Later, when she stopped trying to shape me and she realized it was imposssible to educate me as she would have liked to, she became very nice with me and I think my parents were a little ashamed not to have allowed me to study as I wanted to do. I was very poor, I didn't have a real job – art isn't a job – and so they were ashamed, and Maman tried to do everything she could for me. She was a good woman, but she was still a little girl. She married, she came from a little provincial town and so she could not understand Paris and the world, the new world, and so it was difficult for her.

She didn't have a very happy life. My father was a very bad husband, but she never talked about him. Perhaps it would have been better for her if she had told us. I saw an old friend of hers after her death, and she told me many things. She said, 'Your mother was not happy with your father' – but she never complained. She was very strong. She comes from Lorraine Verdun, and the people there are the toughest in all of France. They are strong people; she was strong but she cried a lot and I couldn't understand why she cried. She cried because she was unhappy and she was poor, without money, and our father kept going away from home, he had a lot of other women. No, she was not a happy woman, but she was always in love with my father and she cried very much when he died.

But I think in fact she was happier after my father's death, because Simone did a lot of things for her and helped her to have a really good life, she could share a beautiful flat, she could travel, and Simone was very generous. I think she was happy.

Simone's book about our mother's death [*A Very Easy Death*] was beautiful, but it was terrible for me to read because it was written not long after she died. But it is very fair, and she

7

wrote many things about my mother that she had not been able to before. It was a revelation, the death of our mother, and Sartre was interested because it revealed another person.

I'm afraid our mother did not find much consolation in religion, she always used to go to mass every day, but when she was dying, she never wanted to see a priest. She didn't want to die and she did not wish to think about death. All the old friends who wanted to see her and help her die, she wouldn't see them. They were sure that Simone and I were wicked women who did not let our mother see her friends, but we said, 'Do you wish to see Madame – ?' and she would say, 'No, no, no!' A priest that she respected very much came to see her – 'No, no, no! When I'm well again.' They all thought it was Simone and I but it wasn't – it was very curious. People are more themselves at this moment.

I always wanted to be a painter. When we were little girls, when we had time, I painted and Simone wrote. I was fascinated by the people I saw from our windows when I was a very little girl – we overlooked the Café Rotonde and I saw much more amusing people than my mother received at home – they seemed happy and amusing and really interesting – people like Modigliani, Picasso . . .

At first I didn't even dare to think I might become a painter – I think I always wanted to, but it seemed impossible, too difficult. Simone was happy about my being a painter because she was like me. We both wished not to have the same life as our mother: this woman who had a very hard life, a very good woman but one who thought only of children, the house, her husband . . . we didn't want that at all.

Simone always helped me in all manner of things, more than morally, she helped me with money. She was a very, very good big sister. She liked looking at paintings, she went to museums and exhibitions and we went to the Musée du Louvre very often together when we were little girls.

I have met a lot of painters, and I have always noticed that great painters were very good to me. Great artists always help you – minor artists are many times wicked and try to put you down. That is normal, I think it's the same everywhere. I even met Picasso, he came to my first exhibition and I was amazed because he told me my work was original. It wasn't original

Simone with Hélène at the opening of
an exhibition of Hélène's paintings

really, because I had seen a lot of paintings at the Musée du Louvre . . . but I did not copy *Picasso*, and at that time nearly all the painters were copying Picasso – so he said mine were 'original'.

It's a great deal more difficult for a woman to be a painter than a man. All my life I have heard 'woman is not creative', and that is a shame because many great painters have been women but history of art doesn't speak about them. It was hard for me, too – not more than for any other woman – but still hard. A friend of mine knew a big collector and she said, 'Oh, you must come and see Hélène de Beauvoir's exhibition.' He said, 'I never see women's exhibitions.'

Simone and I decided not to have children, for several reasons. The first thing was that we did not have a very good relationship with our parents, and we did not wish to have daughters who would talk about us as we sometimes talked about our mother. The other reason is that it is very, very difficult to write important books or to paint important pictures with children.

Some women with children have written, because you can write with just one small table. Perhaps it would be better to have a room for yourself; for instance a friend of ours with a big family used to get up early and go and write in a bar. But a painter needs a lot of space. You see all the room I take up, it's terrible. At one time I just had a little room and a small studio, yet you have so many things – it is a craft.

Being a painter, in a way, made me a feminist before Simone. You see, Simone became a feminist only after she had written *The Second Sex*. She had not suffered by being a woman because she did the same studies as men. She was to be a teacher in a girl's *lycée* (at that time they weren't mixed), so she didn't take the place of a man. But a young painter, a girl who wants to paint, has many occasions to know the worst side of men.

I could tell you many things, but just one example: for my exhibition in 1937 I was still young, but an architect ordered from me two big panels, as high as this room, and I worked hard and in the end I thought they weren't bad. But when he came to collect the panels, there was one condition – you can guess what the condition was. Many times I had that sort of thing, and so you become a feminist.

I liked *The Second Sex* when I first read it. She wrote about so many things I had thought but could not express. She taught me a lot. It is a beautiful book, and it's still considered a very important book about women. Nobody has written a more important book, so modern. She said herself she was a little optimistic about a socialist world being a cure-all for women. That is not true because even if there were a perfect world for men, it would never be a perfect world for women – women have to struggle for themselves.

It does feel strange to be written about, in the way Simone did, and sometimes it is another point of view. But it is always interesting. For example, *Memoirs of a Dutiful Daughter*: I have nothing against it. It is not wrong. As girls we were so. I don't think I ever appeared in her novels. Sometimes I said, 'Why don't you ever show creative women in your novels? A really creative person, a woman who wanted to write and wasn't able to,' but she said, 'I am a creative person, but most women have sad lives, and I show these women.' She chose not to show positive women.

I felt abandoned by Simone twice in my life – but not for long. The first time it was with Zaza, because a girl as young as Simone is not able to pay attention to her little sister and so for some months I hated Zaza. But afterwards she became nice with me and I liked her very much; she was very, very good with me.

When Simone took her first teaching job in Marseilles it was difficult for me and for her – it was terrible to have to go to Marseilles and it was really terrible for me to be left alone in Paris, but we wrote a lot and I went there twice. We walked and walked, we walked along the coast from Marseilles to Toulon, not in one day, but little by little, and it was beautiful. At that time the Côte d'Azur was still so beautiful.

After the war, when Lionel and I were living in Portugal, Simone was invited by the French Institute to come to a conference. The director of the Institute, Pierre Hourcade, was a nice man and he lent us the Institute car. Cars were very few in Portugal, and going through the country with a driver was marvellous. Simone travelled all over Portugal, she did her conference and she was so pleased with it all because she was hungry during the war. When she arrived, well – your parents were the same in London – she arrived with wooden shoes, clothes that were completely rotten and she was so pleased to eat. One day they were quite shocked at the French Embassy (diplomats are sometimes like that). They gave a big lunch for Simone and Simone exclaimed, 'What a beautiful fish!' They thought it was not educated to say 'What a beautiful fish,' but they had eaten always and they did not understand that Simone was a very natural person, she did not try to be discreet, distinguished or anything. I was furious with those diplomats!

I was in fact the one who first went on a rendezvous with Sartre. There's a funny story about how Simone asked me to go and meet him for her. Our friend Mau, the one who called Simone 'Castor', he knew her before Sartre and Sartre was very anxious to get to know Simone. But he asked to meet her, disappointingly, in a little *crèmerie*, not at all nice, it was really not *sympathique*. So Mau told her, 'No, please don't go, I want to introduce you to Sartre myself.' So Simone said, 'I cannot go to that appointment, will you go for me? You go and say to Sartre that you are obliged to go . . .' And I said, 'How shall I know who is Sartre?' She said, 'He wears glasses and he is very, very ugly.' When I went into the *crèmerie*, there were two men with glasses, and Sartre said to me, 'How did you know it was me?' I said, 'Because of the glasses,' but he said, 'So has the other one.' He took me to the cinema but the conversation was very dull. When I returned and everyone said, 'Sartre is so amusing,' I thought, 'He is not amusing at all.' I think he found me very dull, too. Later on, of course, we became very good friends.

I think in fact it was really marvellous they found one another. They helped one another a lot but when people say that Simone owes everything to Sartre (especially French *machistes*), that is not true. Sartre's work owes more to Simone than Simone owes to Sartre, because Sartre was a genius but Simone had great judgment. I never knew a person of such judgment. She went right to the heart of the matter, and that is a very rare quality. Sartre sometimes could be confused, but Simone immediately saw what was wrong. He said he could not have written *La Nausée* without her; they always helped one another a great deal.

When she went to Rouen and met Olga and began writing about the threesome between herself, Olga and Sartre it didn't disturb me at all, because it didn't change anything. Nothing or nobody changed my relationship with Simone, it was too strong.

If you have a sister, you must know that is a special relationship, and so I didn't listen to Olga. I didn't understand her then – I understood much later when I found that Sartre had a real passion for Olga. That explained everything, but I was too young at the time to understand. I thought it was so curious that this little girl was able to turn Sartre's head completely – he, who thought only about his work and thought it was the most important thing. Yet he was so fascinated by her that he began to believe that it was really stupid to think so much about work, that it was beautiful to live like her, without thinking, without willing her to do anything. It was just the contrary of himself and so it was hard for me to understand.

It upset Simone. Simone was not a jealous person, but he took Olga too seriously. Everybody, even young people deserve to be taken seriously. But you don't completely change your life and your way of thinking because of their little fantasy.

But no one really threatened Simone's relationship with him. Some women tried, in America. One day I asked Simone, 'Do you resent a little Sartre's adventures?' She told me, 'It depends on the woman – when they are nice women I don't resent it at all.' But when some women were wicked with her, well, it was natural that she resented it. She was afraid. Freedom is the most beautiful thing but also it is a very difficult thing.

Sartre's death was a terrible blow to Simone. She nearly died, she went to hospital for a fortnight, she couldn't walk any more. She never walked very well again, but she could still walk and I must say that Sylvie helped a lot. Sartre had been everything for her. It was a great help to have someone young who helped her, and did everything for her and she could travel with Sylvie. The first time she came here, to Strasbourg, she always came in October, she liked autumn. Sartre died in April and she came here in October – she was very bad. She said, 'I shall die too.' One year later she was much better and the last years, well, she was never the same, but you can see in the photographs her face was very clear and happy. But sometimes there are things which cannot be repaired.

She died while I was visiting friends in America. Yolande Patterson had organized an exhibition in San Francisco and she wanted Simone to go. Simone said, 'I cannot go, but you go and I shall pay the travelling costs for you.' The day she went into the hospital Sylvie phoned me: 'I have taken Simone to the hospital, **13** she has something like appendicitis.' It wasn't appendicitis, it was something else.

I went to Paris and saw Simone in hospital, and found her in a bad way. I phoned Yolande and told her, 'If I don't find her better tomorrow, I shall not come.' The day after she seemed much better and the doctor said, 'She is much better, you may go.'

So I went to San Francisco and a very nice friend, younger than me, phoned the hospital every day and then let me know in San Francisco how she was getting on. The news was better, so I was very happy. Then one morning Sylvie phoned me that it was finished. It was horrible. Perhaps the most horrible day of my life. But my American friends were marvellous, I never forgot all they did for me on that occasion.

The funeral was extraordinary. My friend Yolande was two hours at the florist's, so many delegations of American women wanted her to give flowers, and there were many African women, Algerian women with enormous bouquets, flowers, and all the women cried, everybody cried. She was very loved. Some men cried too. Lanzmann read some lines by the graveside and the feminists sang a very beautiful French feminist song.

It was very difficult to start painting again. It was such a shock, and my husband was not well. It was very difficult but painting helped me and the first thing I painted was *La Grande Séparation* – it gave me courage, because I did it for Simone.

I had done a portrait of Simone many years ago. An artist had done a portrait of her, very ugly, and she said, 'Why don't you do a portrait of me?' 'Because you never want to pose.' 'Ah, this summer I will come and pose for you.' So I decided to do her portrait again – I looked at my photographs and I have her face in my head, I know it so well.

Simone was the most lively person I ever met. She was so full of life and that was marvellous, and so intelligent, so clever, she really understood everything. She had great judgment, she was very good and generous, really kind. She could not bear to see people unhappy. You couldn't imagine the number of people she helped. She never had a secretary, always answered herself all the letters she received, and I know she received some stupid ones because now I receive some of them. All these people adored her, and she took the time to answer every letter.

14   Until her death, we were old, but I always thought of

myself as 'the little sister'. It was a very good relationship, always *la grande soeur* and *la petite soeur*. For me it was quite normal because I have always known her, she was the first person I knew. As a little girl I adored her. My first memory is when I was three years old, we were out visiting somewhere and I screamed, 'I want to be next to Simone!' I wanted always to be with her, and she was my little protector. She really did protect me, all my life; I always had the impression that as long as I had Simone, nothing would happen to me.

Kate Millett

2
Kate Millett

I was a friend of Simone de Beauvoir's and went to see her every year in Paris. I still think about her. I'm trying to write about her; I don't advance very fast because it's taken me a long time to figure it out. She had an enormous power to be an example, I saw her as much as a teacher as I did a friend – she seemed to have within herself such an unlikely thing, a moral authority... to describe what she was like is not easy. Yes, she was a middle-aged lady who always wore what a friend of mine calls a toque and I call a turban, and she had a very definite voice. She was extremely agreeable and enormously charming, although everyone was scared of her, because she was supposed to be so smart.

Of course, she was a very nice companion, an excellent person and good company and all of those things. But it's much more than that, you know. There was this integrity, if you could boil it down to one word, that was absolute. And if you were with her, it was a touchstone. If you touched base that way once a year, in more or less the same way that going to France can keep an American from going crazy, living in this messed-up country, seeing her once a year made you understand what it was you were doing and why you were doing it. And so the hate-mongers didn't matter, the reactionaries didn't matter, and the factions didn't matter – all that stuff didn't matter. What mattered was the purpose. She reminded you of the purpose. Principally because she had such a beautiful sense of ethics, such a good understanding of politics, such a human view of human activity and human history and human personality.

It was a tonic. It defined, as she and Sartre did together, what it was like to be a human being and to try to be a good human being in this century – that was living existentially, as it were. She represented a great deal to women because she took that position for us and brought about a great deal of our liberation as human beings in this social structure; it would **17** never have been conceivable, let alone achieved, without her ability to conceive all those terms and that condition.

For me, getting to see Simone de Beauvoir was getting to see a famous person, you know. So I'd resort to the horrid little dodges people do. The first time I met her, I had a formal letter of introduction from a man who was her publisher in the United States, who very gallantly offered me this, and she thought it was so silly because she felt as a feminist I could go and see her anyway. I thought that was grand.

But then the next time I'd go back and I would send her flowers and let her know where I was staying, and then if she wanted to see me she could, and I wouldn't be a nuisance. She'd call up and all the people in the hotel would just go insane, because it was Simone de Beauvoir. It was really strange that there could be a country where a writer or intellectual was like, wow, a movie star or royalty or something. The respect that was accorded to her in France – the more you got to know her, the more you realized it still wasn't as good as it should have been, but it was still quite amazing, for an American, to see what intellectuals and writers mean to French people and culture. And the contact that the people have with them, too. They know them the way we would know baseball players over here.

She spent her mornings writing, and then, she loved good food, so she would have a very good lunch – at least the days I saw her, but those may have been days that she took off to have lunch with somebody. She lived always in the same little section, always on the Left Bank, within just a few blocks of everything that she ever did. All her favourite restaurants, the Sorbonne where the libraries were, and the Bibliothèque Nationale, which isn't so far away. And her favourite coffee houses. She was enormously citified, she adored streets, she adored cafés. And I think she probably loved being at home. She lived in one room. I was very impressed that this distinguished person, who'd published a great deal, could have gone and busied themselves a lot with a house in the country and other follies, but instead she just lived in this one big room.

I was full of little questions to ask. I had just published a book and got my name in the paper, and so I had to know how to cope with it all quickly, from someone who'd done all these things. I was thinking in fact of buying this place, I didn't know whether I really should, and she was not going to urge me into property in any big hurry either, because she said that she thought it was silly to own anything, a great deal of nuisance. Her answer to the whole question was, 'Sartre and I go to the same place in Italy every year,' which is not a bad answer really, once you've taken care of things and paid taxes, and worried about broken windows and things like that. Just go some place and pay a hotelier for ten days every year, and call it a vacation. You don't need to get too over-extended.

Her whole life was lived with that kind of economy towards her work. That's what she did. She had such an amazing integrity. You'd meet her and you'd say, hmmmm, the real thing, Simone de Beauvoir. It was in everything in her room – all the photographs were just little photographs, they really were Sartre, Genet, Camus and everybody, on vacation in swimming suits or sitting on the beach or in a café or whatever. They were actual pictures, not the media image, not this historical filter, nothing. One big room lined with books. And these funny sort of fifties-type sofas with velvet cushions that were probably all the rage the year she got it and decorated it. And it had never changed. But that was it. In that room she actually wrote all those books, and had all those thoughts that went to making all those books. It's an enormous achievement, just in terms of literary production. And it was probably all done just because she didn't run around and do anything else.

When Simone de Beauvoir came here to the farm, she came with Sylvie le Bon. I'd always seen de Beavoir in Paris and it was very strange to think she would be in Poughkeepsie. It was very thrilling, too, to have someone that you admire and love so much actually get all the way across the water, at a considerable age, and right into your own house. We had elaborate preparations.

For Simone de Beauvoir to be in Poughkeepsie was surreal – they were driving a car, and they couldn't find the way. So I went to meet them at the Holiday Inn on Highway Nine, because that was the only place they could be sure of finding. It was an enormous cultural transplantation for the two of them to be at the Holiday Inn. I didn't quite believe they could be there until I got to the parking lot. I led them back here, and they stayed for about five days. It was the nicest way to be with a friend, because you see each other all the way round the clock and you have one meal after another, not just one visit a year.

It kind of blessed the place, that she was here. And she understood and sympathized with everything we were trying to do. I think she liked it a lot, and she liked what we were doing here, with the colony. That surprised me too in a sense – one thinks of her as the existential, independent model of the first generation of women, you know, transcending everything in culture and history and making it on their own, being their own selves and so forth. *The Second Sex* dealt with all of our history up to that point, and set us on our course. But it was not concerned with the political organization of women very much, nor with the creation of a women's movement. When the second wave of feminism did occur in France, many years after that book was published, she was very involved with, and very happy about the emergence of the French women's movement. But she'd been all alone out there for many, many years.

What we were doing in the colony was still a different sort of thing – we're living communally, in a band or a group, a colony of artists, not like those feminist pioneer women artists or writers, say, such as herself or Nevilson or Virginia Woolf, who lived difficult isolated lives.

I didn't know how she would cotton on to this. But she liked it very much – she had such faith in our little Utopian scheme that it was very heartening to us. It was the early time here and this place was a wilderness. We had to restore lands that hadn't been used for a very long time. It was exhausting and heroic and impossible, enough to kill you. So having her here smiling serenely over the whole project for five days made us take heart and believe in our own fantasies, which she gave a great deal of reality to.

When I read *The Second Sex* I was at Oxford; I read it shortly after it came out. It was a very disturbing book. In fact, early editions often had nude ladies on the cover and it almost had a sort of mischievous cachet. Apparently it was so subversive that it got mixed up with being a little sexy too. You were a real firebrand if you read that book, and if you paid any attention to it, you were – you know, all the awful things you tried so hard not to be: a castrating bitch or not satisfied with your fate or in need of a therapist or something. People fought about that book all the time.

I had friends at the Sorbonne, so I spent all my six-week

Kate Millett in the sixties
Picture © Granada Publishing

Oxford vacations in Paris – I was going to the Sorbonne kind of on the side, with my Sorbonne friends. They argued about that book all the time. The ones at Oxford did too, but you know, Parisian arguments are a lot more passionate, and it was the city where the existentialists flourished; you were really aware of people caring a great deal about these ideas. We'd sit in cafés and eat the sugar for free, and scream about the ideas all afternoon.

The Second Sex made a great deal of sense to me. It was a siren call to a lot of other people, and a very dangerous book. This book could change your life, it could make you dissatisfied. It could make you not just want to be one of the good girls that went to college, but you wanted to kick the windows in too.

You challenged everything then, and that meant you challenged everything you read and everything in the courses, and the purpose and shape of your own life. It took hold of you, it did for a lot of women my age. It really did change their lives. After that, we never saw things the same way.

I owe a great debt to *The Second Sex*. I couldn't have written *Sexual Politics* without it, without the philosophic and historical perspective that de Beauvoir gives to the condition of women, or the way you are inside your own mind – the way you exist not only socially and culturally but also the way you imagine you exist. She defined all of that, brilliantly. Since the Renaissance there's been text after text that has taken the condition of women or the relationship between the sexes and just blown them sky high. But this book did it in the language of my time, and it did it with such scope and circumference.

What I wanted to do, though, was different. De Beauvoir really deals with the inner perception of the feminine condition. Women are '*les autres*' – the others; the human condition is male. That is, men, being in power, have decided that the human condition is what they are and we're something else. But since she's dealing so much with psychology and self-perception, sometimes it gets a little vague whether it's really this way or whether it's that way because it was expedient to set things up this way or that – the idea was really power control.

Well, I wanted to have a structural analysis of how an institution, namely patriarchy, works. I'm really much more interested in the politics than the psychology. It's a difference in perspective and approach. I wanted to lay out how an institution, which is in fact a political institution, is involved with power all the way along the line – whether it's about money, guns, who's God, what sex is God, who runs the family, who decides about the laws, who holds political or inherited office, and who exercises force and who has money.

I'm involved with power – that's what politics is all about – and so I dealt with politics on a much more institutional level than she did. But if she hadn't broken the veil and shed some light on what was a very taken-for-granted, assumed situation, I couldn't have done what I did. It was absolutely basic to have that as a stepping stone. It's a glorious, big, very learned, very wonderful book, full of light.

I think de Beauvoir realized that I probably cribbed a whole lot more in what I was doing, all my politics through literature – cultural criticism I called it. I had a section on D. H. Lawrence which was, I now realize, painfully indebted to her analysis of Lawrence in *The Second Sex*. I didn't re-read the book when I wrote *Sexual Politics*, but I did re-read that section and I did say 'thank you' at one point or another. Now I realize that I was probably cheating all over the place, and owed a great deal to what she had said. Or maybe to the confidence with which she had said it. I think she almost felt that I didn't give her enough credit there. I was dealing with an English writer, and had this wonderful insight into how to read Lawrence, yet she was the first person who published it when she put it in *The Second Sex*. She often sort of scolded me about that. Justly, too.

De Beauvoir was taking on the psychologists, largely. There's a great deal about Freud and Kraft-Ebbing and all these folks in *The Second Sex* because she's doing a philosophic existentialist analysis of what are the received opinions of the inner scope of certain groups, males and females, and what is feminity, what is masculinity. She had to go to the classic psychological literature. And she had to very gently and sweetly contradict it all, which had enormous power. What Friedan described in *The Feminine Mystique*, a lot of the reaction that followed suffrage and re-instituted female passivity came through psychology, you know. It was a very reactionary force in this particular circumstance.

So if you set out to do anything about this, you have to deal with the psychologists, because they're the authorities. And she did, at great length. They are very tedious people to deal with, **23** it's all a labyrinth of language and jargon, belief systems and myths. If you fall for the Oedipus complex, you can be thrashing around in a paper bag called 'Theory of the Oedipus Complex' for a very long time. It's a means of perceiving knowledge which must have been pretty hard for a French existential philosopher to deal with, but she did not get stuck in psychological theory. She could break out of the endless paper bags and bring some light on to things.

A lot of feminist analysis is still thumping against the walls of Freudian theory: what is abnormal sexuality, what is sexual liberation, you know, on and on. Her chapter on lesbians says some very nice things – these are autonomous, independent women. And she's into their having quite a variety of ways of being and lifestyles. But she's still sort of stuck with the classical psychological descriptions of these people, those weird words like 'vaginal' or 'cliteroid', or 'masculinist' women, terms that nobody even uses any more. Behind that are all Kraft-Ebbing's or Freud's theories. Lesbians are still observed as shades of abnormal psychology, and it is very quaint when you read it.

Simone de Beauvoir's relationship with French feminism was a strange one. She'd been the prophet crying in the wilderness for about twenty years between the publication of *The Second Sex* and the beginning of the second wave of feminism in France. All that time she'd been the personification of that dreadful idea, feminism, and was much abused for writing this book, even by her friends, by Camus for example, and that hurt her very much. Throughout the world she stood for this anathema, feminism.

When there was an organized political movement in the United States and France and elsewhere, much younger women were involved with it. They also came out of the New Left in 1968 and all that sort of thing in Paris. They came to it with a different set of assumptions and they already knew how to demonstrate.

One of the first things that happened was that they protested against the laws forbidding abortion. De Beauvoir and a number of other women signed statements that they had broken the law, and had had abortions. In this first action she joined them, and took all the risks. But there was always going to be a generational difference, and she was also a famous person, and their ideology was against all famous people. It was rigidly democratic. The difference of twenty years meant a lot, too. There were moments when you would see the French women's movement finding it convenient to use de Beauvoir as their figure-head, and then privately this or that faction might be saying, 'Oh, well, hmmm . . .' I think this was very painful to her at times, to be used as a *vedette* as she called it, a star, and then trashed as one, or treated with all the usual youthful arrogance or envy.

Yet at the same time I think that her political involvement with the women's movement in France was one of the big excitements of the last years of her life. This gave her, finally, her own cause to be involved with. It had a very good effect on her life, and certainly was a great help to the French women's movement. But it was a difference not just of ages but of generations and styles, a little bit sad too, sometimes. I wished she could have been more directly involved and more surrounded by comrades and sisters than she appeared to be, and less by criticism and isolation.

There are two ways in which de Beauvoir's autobiography has helped me as a writer of autobiography. One is through her memoirs, which we all know – *Memoirs of a Dutiful Daughter*, *The Prime of Life* and *All Said and Done*. For a lot of women of my generation, not just myself, this whole chronicle of her life was the only public life of another woman that we knew was directly autobiographical as opposed to, say, Doris Lessing's fictionalized autobiography – also very useful to us. We needed very much a picture of how someone was doing it, how they were living, how were they becoming these realized independent women. What were their lives really like? Not just our tiny little miniature lives from graduate school and so forth. Here was an example of people who would let us in to their charmed circle and give us a notion of the obstacles they dealt with, and how hard it was for them. They were all innovating – certainly she innovated enormously in her relationship with Sartre. It's an image for this whole century, probably – like Héloïse and Abelard – of these two lovers, comrades, friends, who maintained a relationship over the whole course of a life by never marrying, by never living together. Well, that was the new way to run your life. Her autobiography represented being let in to somebody's fantastic, vital life, somebody who is all the things one would fantasize being. **25**

The other book that comes to mind, though, is the book about her mother's death, *A Very Easy Death*. The record in her memoirs is candid in lots of ways, but it still has an almost official capacity. I mean, it's always describing the war, the occupation and the Resistance – there is always this public spectacle – and also she's dealing with a circle of people who were the great lights of her time. In *A Very Easy Death* it's just her mother dying in hospital, just Simone and her mother, and her mother's cancer, which is so boring and awful and takes so long and is so painful to watch. You have to deal with the fact that you hate the disease because it's consuming your mother, but also because it's so awfully tedious and banal. She is completely honest about this and doesn't spare herself or her mother anything. It's a beautiful piece of writing and a beautiful piece of self-understanding.

A Woman Destroyed, too, is a spectacular piece of fictional writing. It's got such force. We think of her primarily as a writer of memoirs, a historian. But this is very exciting writing, as language and psychology too. It's a study in jealousy that is absolutely brilliant. It's a collection of three short stories; the last one is called 'A Woman Destroyed', but they're all about obsessive jealousy. As you read them you see this character disintegrate. You're in her consciousness day after day, and she completely falls apart – her sense of reality, her sense of self. You experience everything that jealousy does to you: disappointment, being abandoned. It's one of the best studies of this in any language I know.

I read it when I was writing *Sita*, because she was taking a lot of chances I wanted to take, and it's always very good for you as a writer if you come upon another writer who has really gone over the edge of the cliff and is calling up to you from the beach, saying, it's all right. The way in which jealousy or abandonment disintegrates personality, how, as the song says, 'I fall to pieces', she describes so beautifully in *A Woman Destroyed*. It gave me courage to explore and dare to write down feelings that were all part of the experience of *Sita*.

The book *Old Age* is probably ultimately going to be as important as *The Second Sex*. It's just as revolutionary, it's just as obnoxious a message. It disturbs the status quo tremendously, it alerts us to the fact that we're kidding ourselves, and we're treating old people like invisible people or animals or lesser beings. Their response to that generally is to pretend that they aren't old, or to pretend that they don't exist.

It makes us deal with the inhumanity, not only of our treatment of the aged, but of the fact that age is part of the whole: you're young, you're middle-aged, and then you're old – that's part of your life. You're not less young; you're old. If we could come to terms with that, we would live much better lives, I think. It's a very subversive book, and I think it's going to make a lot of difference over time.

> Buddha recognized his own fate in the person of a very aged man, because, being born to save humanity, he chose to take upon himself the entirety of the human state. In this he differed from the rest of mankind, for they evade those aspects of it that distress them. And above all they evade old age. The Americans have struck the word death out of their vocabulary – they speak only of 'the dear departed': and in the same way they avoid all reference to great age. It is a forbidden subject in present-day France, too. What a furious outcry I raised when I offended against this taboo at the end of *La Force des choses*! Acknowledging that I was on the threshold of old age was tantamount to saying that old age was lying there in wait for every woman, and that it had already laid hold upon many of them. Great numbers of people, particularly old people, told me kindly or angrily but always at great length and again and again, that old age simply did not exist! There were those who were less young than others, and that was all it amounted to. Society looks upon old age as a kind of shameful secret that it is unseemly to mention.

> from *Old Age*

I did of course want to meet Sartre, and I was very thrilled because every time we'd have lunch, Simone would suggest it. (I don't think of her always as Simone, I thought of her as S. de B., a sort of code-word between me and my friends, and it's also what you write when you take notes as a scholar. I didn't really think of her as Simone until very much nearer the end of her life, maybe when she stayed here, and then also in her dying – I became far closer to her than I would have otherwise.) Anyway, she'd say, 'Well, next time we'll have lunch with Sartre,' and I'd   **27**

say 'Oh, good,' . . . like I'm going to get introduced to the great
Jean-Paul Sartre and this would be wonderful, I can tell my
friends when I get back. But also it's intimidating to have lunch
with Sartre, so I wasn't ecstatically eager. A little bit scared of
him – had we all read *Being and Nothingness* with sufficient
attention, you know.

It would be all right, it would be next time, and it would be
an added wonderment to seeing her again. But it never
happened. The time it really was definitely going to be, his
funeral had taken place a month before. I was sorry never to
have met him because he meant a great deal to me as a writer as
well, of course. But I always loved those lunches when it was just
us, and our dinners. I liked having that friendship just with her
rather than with the great miraculous duo, which I think people
always tended to see them as being.

And yet sometimes I do have dinner with them. I call it a
way of practising my French. I make up their lines, and it's
enormously entertaining . . . We always have a very witty good
time, and no one notices my grammatical errors. When you
have read that much of people's books, you see, and when they
have been so much part of your life, they are often having dinner
with you, whether you know it or not. If you've been a student
when they were the reigning intellectuals – they were forces,
ideas were that important, it was all that exciting – well, you end
up almost shaping your life by the way they live theirs, by the
ethic they represented.

We all imitated this Sartre–de Beauvoir relationship, as
hard as we could. But never with such resounding success. I
think it did help and made more wonderful the relationships
that I had. But you see, we didn't obey the rules – we did live
together, then the immigration laws forced us to marry. To
maintain what they were trying to do is very romantic and very
wonderful. It was very logical. They were trying to maintain a
long-term fidelity, together with variety. You usually have one
or the other in life. But they wanted to have both, and they could
only do that if they were separate and autonomous entities. That
way they could have other lovers, and they could always be true
to each other over time, instead of serial monogamy – you know,
this decade it's A, this decade it's B. I hardly even remember,
now that I'm with C, where A lives or what his middle name
was. We don't speak any more, we've argued – people really

make such a mess out of these great intimacies. Sartre and de Beauvoir had a great sense of how important that kind of intimacy was, probably because with them it was so entire, it was as much an intellectual as it was a physical affair. You take it with enormous seriousness, far more than people do marriage.

But for de Beauvoir it was also important to have other loves as well, other relationships, though never as important as Sartre. That was achieving a kind of balance so you didn't ask too much of one person. There were other flavours, and other experiences, which other people represented, people of other ages or nationalities.

I think de Beauvoir gives two things to other women. One is a sense of example. There she is in Paris, living this life. She's the brave, independent spirit, she's writ large what I would like to be, here in Podunk. And the other thing is that she gives a woman's life a sense of adventure. She broke a lot of rules. She was a well-bred bourgeois lady and she just did what she liked and came into enormous conflict with her family. Then she lived with Sartre, she refused to marry – an enormous decision, especially in those times. She had awful little teaching jobs, and when she got past them and had enough to survive just from writing, she lived in crummy hotels. She really never had any money, a really good job, a professorship. She was anathema after writing *The Second Sex*. She defied the government and was probably liable to arrest all during the Algerian War. *Le Temps Moderne* – the magazine – was raided by the cops all the time, and they'd take the copies away. They were subversive. It was a much riskier business than being against the war in Vietnam. She and Sartre were at the very centre of the opposition. In every respect she defied convention, all the way along.

Now, when you go to France, Simone de Beauvoir is a person of enormous distinction – a great cultural hero. But that's after sixty years of kicking respectability in the teeth, and it didn't start out that way at all. What both of them represented was the adventure of trying to lead an ethical life, trying to live according to a radical ethical politics, which isn't just the Leftist bible – you have to invent situation ethics all the time. And that's an adventure.

I think that de Beauvoir's life is very much an exemplary life, it's a life of action, of living out for women everywhere. It's **29** taught us a great deal, and that's a very big gift. It's a little more than the books, even.

Her funeral was terribly sad, but it was also triumphant in a way, because so many women came. Funerals in France are sort of public demonstrations of philosophical principles. It was the same at Sartre's funeral in the adoration that culture showed at the time of his death – an enormous respect. De Beauvoir's funeral was like that for French feminism and for French women in general. It was a public occasion, social history, and it was very interesting because of the other participants – you have this great collective grief which you share with all the people who loved her. You're all brothers and sisters.

My own experience of her dying was somewhat different. For some reason I was permitted to go to the morgue, which is certainly not something I would generally wish to do, but in this case I was so disappointed because I couldn't see her – I was in Paris when she was ill, and she was too sick to see anybody. I kept thinking 'She'll get better, I'll show up with my yellow tulips again and it'll be swell.'

But it never happened; suddenly she was dead. It was overwhelming. The family were very kind and let me go to the morgue. I went by myself, one of three permitted to go. There was an official staring at me all the time, very upset that I might take a photograph. I spent the afternoon staring at her profile. I was astonished . . . it was like dealing with the profile on a coin, or a sculpture or something, because she was both the person I knew and she was also now a great French philosopher, part of history. It was a very private experience. It was extremely puzzling, because it was very tender and intimate, and yet at the same time she had become a great figure, part of French culture and civilization.

After the funeral we went back to the Simone de Beauvoir Audio-Visual Centre. Feminists from lots of different countries were there, many of them old friends who'd been in the movement up to their necks for a long time. We began to understand that we had now all grown up. We had lost our mentor, the person from the older generation who knew how. Now we would have to know how. It was like losing your parents and your professor all at once, plus the person who has the key – the one who can read the foreign language, has the map, and knows enough history and politics to dope it out.

It was a coming of age. This great pioneer, the one who'd led the way, wasn't there any more. Yet at the same time she was now inside all of us to an extent. We'd have to find the way through, consolidating everything that she had already taught us. Now we were going to have to remember it – and become it.

Jenny Turner

3
Jenny Turner

I first read Simone de Beauvoir when I was about fifteen or sixteen. Before then I had never heard of her at all. I was still at school, I was very confused indeed, I couldn't make up my mind if I was a punk rocker or mod or modette. I find it hard to remember back to that time but I know that my world seemed very small. Being an adolescent I was totally involved in little dramas with my friends and little dramas with my family. I was trying to rebel but not doing very well at it. I didn't have the guts to get kicked out of school or anything, but what I used to do was go home to my parents and say, 'I think I'm going to leave school now. I don't think I'm going to do any studying, I don't think I'll take my exams', and wait for a reaction. I didn't get one so I'd try again. I was looking hard for a way of rebelling that suited me.

Then I read *The Prime of Life*, which was given to me by my brother's godmother. She was going through some books to be thrown out and gave me some of them, so I read this one. It sounds really corny, but it opened up to me a way of asserting myself that suited me. I didn't have to leave school, which was fine, because I didn't really want to anyway; I could do it the other way around – go full steam ahead and work really hard and that could also be a rebellion. So that's what I started to do.

Going to university was never really an issue – my mother went to university and she wanted all of us to go to university and get a good job. It was my decision to leave Aberdeen and go to Edinburgh, which I wanted to do partly to leave home, and partly because the world did seem such a terribly small place. I had a lot of ideas about culture, about the world, in that sort of existentialist way – the world was something which you choose to enter into. By going to Edinburgh, I thought this was me entering it. So off I went, all in black; it was a bit different to what I had expected.

At the beginning of *The Prime of Life* the image is of this woman moving into a house by herself, her grandmother's lodging house, getting her own room, buying her own bits of furniture, being a philosopher, wearing these strange dark dresses and going to cafés. When I went to Edinburgh this was the sort of stuff that was running through my mind. I had a strange sort of purple hat, which was the nearest thing I could get to a turban. I decided I wanted to study philosophy, because I had heard that de Beauvoir had studied philosophy and it sounded interesting. I really didn't know anything about it at all. As it happened, I took English and Philosophy and ended up dropping philosophy then picking it up later on.

What I think is interesting in all this is the way I was being drawn into and influenced by a sort of myth, the existentialist myth maybe, the bit about Paris, the Left Bank, cafés, etc. This is the very common superficial response I think – attraction to the glamour – but there are still aspects of it worth looking at seriously. For instance, one of the things visitors always find depressing about Britain is the absence of public life, of cafés and cheap restaurants. I think it makes it harder to make a life writing or reading or thinking, this absence of public life. There is a bit in *Force of Circumstance* where Simone de Beauvoir talks about how she and Sartre went to Edinburgh, which is where I live, and they only stay two days because they cannot bear it. They ask for a cup of tea and the landlady says, 'You can't have a cup of tea, it's after breakfast time.' They are not allowed to sit in their rooms during the day, they are not allowed to work in their rooms. That sort of dourness, also the refusal to let you forget for a moment there is a price tag attached to everything you think you're doing for pleasure. I'm sure it originated in Britain, the practice of landladies charging extra for a bath, and one of the things that gets young Brits excited about continental travel is the hope and belief that things over there are simpler and warmer – a naïvety, but you can see where it comes from.

Another aspect of the existentialist myth is the seriousness and lack of surprise with which Simone de Beauvoir treats her destiny as an intellectual. I think it's easy to misunderstand de Beauvoir and Sartre – to see them as po-faced and self-important in thinking of themselves as intellectuals, that way of thinking or speaking not being native to this country at all. It is more natural in their language, but still not the most obvious thing to be. And it's not obvious how to go about it. It sounds very self-important to talk about being an intellectual, especially in Britain, but there's no reason why this should be foreign to us. An intellectual is not a stock figure, like the man selling onions with the beret and stripy shirt. I suppose I try to be an intellectual, and it's very hard, not only to be one but to work out what it is you're trying to do in the first place.

This myth, these images that attract people initially, this still goes on today. A couple of weeks ago I was in a bar in the Highlands. There was a bunch of kids of about sixteen who were all drunk and trying to wind me up. It's a long story, but one came up to me and put his arms on my shoulder and said, 'What do you think is the relevance of existentialism in the modern world?' I gave him a straight answer – he was upset about that, he didn't want a straight answer, he just wanted to wind me up. But what I thought was interesting was that the myth, the glamour, that was getting people going in the fifties and sixties, and seventies in my case, still seems to get them going today. I'm sure it's a fairly middle-class phenomenon, middle-class kids with some sort of an aspiration, but the young bourgeoisie have to escape from bourgeois structures in order to think. And they have to be able to think in order to contribute usefully to the world instead of lining their pockets, so this influence is very important.

There's a lot of self-importance, and a lot of ostentation involved in taking oneself seriously as an intellectual, but it seems to me to be a good way to start.

There's a sort of promise in it: that you can belong to the world in this existential, ethical way and you don't have to stop getting excited about things when you cease to be a child. There's the promise, as well, of the 'good life' in a political sense; you know, you're going to be a lefty and it's going to be nice, there's going to be nice food, a good time, good friends, travel, the whole world opening up. All these things are held out as a promise in the autobiographies, and to an extent in the novels as well. Yet at the end of *Force of Circumstance* de Beauvoir sees this is an illusion, a con – she looks back at herself as a young woman, hoping for and expecting so much from life, seeing no contradiction between the pursuit of personal pleasure and a struggle for social change. She thinks that she has actually got most of what she wants and realizes it means nothing, it's a complete swindle. It still seems to me a fairly good attitude to go

above
Jenny Turner as a child

above left
Jenny (right foreground) on a
family holiday

centre left
At home in Aberdeen

below left
Graduation day

opposite page (above)
Jenny (middle) with friends

below
On a climbing holiday in the
Highlands

into adult life with, a sort of necessary illusion if you like; maybe you need to dream of the good life in order to be able to keep going.

I don't think she has been a role model as such. I don't think I have ever thought, Simone de Beauvoir did this, therefore I must do this. I mean, I have a friend for whom she is very much of a role model, in a lighthearted sort of way – she wears a turban and everything and went to Marseilles on her holidays and ended up nearly killing herself by falling down a mountain because that was where Simone de Beauvoir climbed in *The Prime of Life*. There is a level on which female role models are important for women but that's very different from holding one woman to account because you happen to go for her ideas or her work or the way she dresses. One-to-one role-model relationships – if they exist to the extent that writers say they do, which I doubt – are a nonsense, a very silly and limiting way to spend your life, very self-regarding and self-absorbed.

I suppose I think of Simone de Beauvoir as a special sort of friend. You can have a friendship but you don't copy your friends, you're not influenced by them in the same way as by a hero or heroine or role model. You don't get these rather silly questions about was she right, was she telling the truth. You don't ask your friends to be right, or if they are telling the truth about their self-image. Who cares? The point is what they make of it. Somewhere in *Force of Circumstance* a lassie comes to see Simone de Beauvoir – it is one of those friendships with younger women she so often had – and she says to this woman, 'Don't go around getting yourself heroes and heroines, they will only disappoint you.' It's a very unrealistic way of looking at the world.

Every year there are certain books I read over and over again. Once a year at least, whenever I go home to see my parents, oftener in times of distress. The main book is *Anne of Green Gables* and it struck me that de Beauvoir's autobiography is very much a grown-up, sceptical version of *Anne of Green Gables*. The optimism is the same, the making the most of bad things, the determination to see things through. After *Anne*, I read the travel bits in *The Prime of Life*. Then *Memoirs of a Dutiful Daughter* – it's the easy one, all food and clothes and meeting your boyfriend, great. I've graduated now to enjoying *Force of Circumstance* too. You go back to them again and again, they fall open at the same bits.

When I re-read this quite recently, it became clear to me that Simone de Beauvoir never really wanted to write about the world, all she wanted to do was eat it, and her whole philosophy seems to come from this moment:

> the world became more intimately part of me when it entered through my mouth than through my eyes and sense of touch. I would not accept it entirely. The insipidity of milk puddings, porridge and mashes of bread and butter made me burst into tears; the oiliness of fat meat and the clammy mysteries of shellfish revolted me; tears, screams, vomitings: my repugnance was so deeply rooted that in the end they gave up trying to force me to eat those disgusting things. On the other hand, I eagerly took advantage of that privilege of childhood which allows beauty, luxury and happiness to be things that can be eaten . . .

from *Memoirs of a Dutiful Daughter*

It's all there – the linking of ideas with feeling, with eating, with that tremendous zest and enthusiasm for life. De Beauvoir never struggled to make a living as a writer. She worked as a teacher, into her thirties. When Sartre started making money she was supported by him, then when her own books started doing well she got her money that way, so she never struggled to make a living as a writer, which I think was very sensible because it can do strange things to your perspective. She does talk about a sort of artistic struggle, about how long it took her to find something to write about, and you wonder if the reason she embarked upon the autobiographies was because she found fiction just too hard to do.

I like the autobiography best because I don't think she's a great writer; apart from *The Mandarins* I don't think I have ever finished one of her novels. *The Mandarins* I think is an interesting book, it is very much a companion to *Force of Circumstance*, they are different ways of rendering the same experience. I find her fiction often cumbersome and self-important, characters representing philosophical positions, that sort of uninspired and very bourgeois ethos. She's a very workman-like – workperson-like – writer, her style is not interesting and you get the feeling she wrote it by the yard.

She talks in the autobiographies about drafting and   **39** redrafting, about working really hard on her book, but I don't believe her. What I like so much about the autobiographies is there is very little premeditation, they are formless and wander here and there. They are enormous volumes, 400–600 pages long, three big ones, one shorter one, a huge amount to get through, and very little art to them. I like this roughness, and the ponderousness with which they take you, step by step, through how decisions were made or whatever. I find them very useful, very supportive. Their dullness – their cosy bulk – is useful in a crisis as well as the actual bits of advice.

Force of Circumstance is the book I think about the most at the moment. I was completely grabbed by the sense in it of history being lived through. I would be surprised if there were a finer account anywhere of the Algerian War as it was actually happening, as it looked to people in Paris. *Force of Circumstance* opens with elation at the liberation of Paris in 1945. You get the amazing sense at the beginning of the book that de Beauvoir and her friends actually believe that their deliberations about the world are crucial, because they are going to achieve real political power. They genuinely thought, having been part of the Resistance, part of the triumphant anti-fascist movement, that they were going to have considerable power in the new France – in postwar Europe, the Europe talked about in *The Mandarins* as a third way, half-way between the United States and the Soviet Union. As it happened they were wrong, De Gaulle came back and there was that terrible period when France seemed to be collapsing under another sort of very simple politics, very close to fascism, at the time of the Algerian Revolution. This is when Simone de Beauvoir gave up expecting her promise to be fulfilled. She writes about it as a time of great disillusionment for herself.

I never noticed this until quite recently – the terrible sense of a whole world collapsing, which hits Simone de Beauvoir with the Occupation of France, when she visits Berlin, during the Algerian War. It's really valuable, I think, to take note of this, because a lot of people talk about how they want to be politically committed, to think and act globally, to have some sort of global consciousness, yet at the same time they lead a very secure and comfortable life, which is an insoluble contradiction. You have this problem of material security versus the tremendous his-torical insecurity of the world. What the autobiography shows is that it isn't really a contradiction at all – because there is no such thing as being definitely secure, your world might fall apart at any moment and the trick is not to try to hide from this but to accept it and act accordingly. The Second World War hit Simone de Beauvoir when she was about thirty, just when her life should have been getting very cosy, as she was beginning to get a bit self-satisfied. Then suddenly all of it disintegrates. I've never experienced that – in western Europe people born after the war haven't – but it's part of everyday life for the people of eastern Europe, and in most of the rest of the world: maybe you can't even depend on a national boundary still being there in the morning, and it's tremendously important for people to grasp that the world could fall apart at any time. We should think and act accordingly – none of us are as secure as we'd like to think we are.

A lot of the self-consciously feminist biographies that have come out in the last few years are very clearly but superficially influenced by de Beauvoir, by her example in her autobiographies, by the particular way she puts questions of commitment, things like that. I find them a bit dull because they never seem to talk about anybody apart from themselves really, everything is seen in relation to themselves and to the question of their identity – 'my freedom', 'my independence', and so on. This theme is very minor in de Beauvoir's own work. It may be an initial attraction but most of her writing is committed to things outside herself and I especially like the way she wrote about her friendships. She was so interested in her friends and stuck by them a long time. To an extent they look like a surrogate family; didn't she call them 'the family' for a while?

People tend to get a bit knowing at this point, as if the creation of a surrogate family has to be a replacement for the loss of a 'real' family, whereas I don't think it was a surrogate at all. It may be a really interesting way to start thinking about rebuilding a life, independent lives, that aren't based on jealousy and possessiveness, manipulation, all the things that couples and nuclear families get into.

I think if you got a computer to do an analysis of the autobiographies, you'd find that quantitatively there is a lot less about Sartre than people tend to think. People adopt the couple, the heterosexual drama as the centrepiece because that is convention. But there's an enormous amount about her other **41** friends, about her devotion to her sister, about Zaza obviously, but also about many other friends that we come back to again and again. I would hope, I suppose, that has been an influence. I would hope I take my friends seriously, anyway, but I do think our culture is biased against friendship. Maybe Simone de Beauvoir is a pioneer in this respect.

For younger women reading her today, I think one of Simone de Beauvoir's charms – one of the really fine things – is that she wrote an enormous amount of stuff, she was into quantity over quality and I think that's a good attitude to have. She wrote novels, she wrote essays, she wrote philosophy, history, she wrote *The Second Sex*. Nowadays people specialize. It is fashionable to produce the odd slim volume or a TV programme with a very narrow perspective – part of the trendifying of philosophy and selected leftish ideas in this country over the last few years. De Beauvoir's sort of earnestness over elegance is an example of a different way of going about things. An idea that curiosity is the important thing and that you can't afford to dismiss anything if you really want to find out about the world we live in.

I find a lot of the books written by modern feminists frustrating for these reasons. I find them narrow and self-absorbed, navel-watching and a bit timid. They are written quickly and rely too much on a shared knowledge of shibboleth. Many of them seem to me to lack a sense of history. They don't look outside themselves to other possibilities. In that respect I think it's brilliant to go back to the work of someone like Simone de Beauvoir, who couldn't just mention a women's movement in her writing and take it for granted that her readers knew what she was talking about.

De Beauvoir's work may help feminist thought to move on because it is so unhampered, it is independent work, she was at her time doing something very new and fresh. Nothing is taken for granted in *The Second Sex*. Of course a lot of *The Second Sex* is practically unreadable now, because it seems so full of platitudes. But they weren't platitudes then, they took great courage to write. That's the sort of courage women need to find again, to look at everything afresh. We can't take anything for granted, everything is up for grabs.

Margaret Walters

4
Margaret Walters

I was brought up in Australia, and when I was a student somebody lent me a copy of *The Mandarins*. It was about 1960, and I had never heard of Simone de Beauvoir. I read it and I was terribly impressed by this high-powered intellectual novel about something that was literally half a world away from me, about politics in France after the Second World War. But it was also a 'woman's novel' in the old-fashioned sense. The emotional power of the novel, which I found very haunting then and still do now, is the heroine's unhappy affair with an American writer, and I was very intrigued by that.

I found I remembered it when I came to England, and at some point in the early sixties I came across *The Second Sex* and read that, and again it really hit me very hard. I think I must have been unsure of what I was doing at Oxford and didn't like it much; I was feeling isolated and not very happy, and the book suddenly fell into place.

It's fascinating looking back, but I had never actually read any feminist texts before. I was quite well educated but I had never realized that there was a lot of theoretical writing in existence about what it is to be a woman. This was the first feminist book that I ever read, and it was very important. I found myself continually going back to it and re-reading it; that whole notion of woman as 'other' worked as a hook for all sorts of problems. It helped me make more sense of my own dissatisfactions, as I later found out it did for many other women. It talked about woman's situation, what it meant to be a woman, what women could be, in general terms, and I found that very exciting.

During the sixties the autobiographies and novels were being published in English and I read them as they came out. Again that was a very interesting experience because you felt you had a growing intimacy with someone. At that point I also started to realize how connected all her work was, that the theory and the autobiography and the novels were all intensely personal, they were all reflecting, saying something about her life, and I did get very intrigued by that.

I think one of the interesting things about the autobiographies is their clarity; it is an incredibly detailed self-portrait done with enormous confidence. It's about one woman's quest for freedom and she presents herself as finding it. It's a success story, and it's enormously consistent, from the first of her *Memoirs of a Dutiful Daughter* right through to *All Said and Done* – there is total consistency. What intrigued me from the beginning, though, was the sense of a shadow behind that clarity and confidence. She touches on areas that are more disturbing and contradictory, and then, to some extent, she retreats from them. She's got an amazing way of raising emotions like jealousy or anger or pain or loneliness, and then shutting off, denying they were very important in her life.

But in the novels she did explore those things. She admits that *L'Invitée* (*She Came to Stay*), the first real book that she wrote, grew out of a period when she was very unhappy, the first time she had to ask questions about her relationship with Sartre. She and Sartre had both become extremely involved with a young student called Olga but it was Sartre who called the tune, and de Beauvoir found herself very confused and miserable. She wrote *L'Invitée* out of that confusion and it's a most extraordinary book because it explores in an enormously powerful way – I must have read it half a dozen times and it still affects me – what jealousy is really like; and also anger. In a way it's a revenge story where the heroine actually ends up murdering the woman who is her rival.

The extraordinary thing in the novel, and I think it's very characteristic of de Beauvoir, is that the philosophical structure of the book is optimistic, rational, all to do with 'self' and the 'other'. And de Beauvoir actually finds an intellectual justification for the heroine killing the younger girl. But the emotional effect of the novel is quite different. It's about the heroine's anger towards the man and towards the young girl, and about her vengeance – which quite literally becomes murderous. I think it's a very important book because it explores this taboo, dark area.

People reading the books often thought of her and Sartre as a sort of ideal couple. I think we all probably had a tendency to glamorize them, particularly in the sixties. The whole question **45**

top
Margaret Walters as a child in Australia

bottom
With her father on graduation day

opposite page
On a trip to Paris during which she visited
Simone de Beauvoir at her flat

of her relationship with Sartre is a difficult one – right from the beginning she says it is the central thing in her life: she says Sartre provided her with that sense of total safety that previously she had only got from her parents or from God. She actually says that he guaranteed happiness for her, he justified her whole life for her. She then admits that she couldn't do the same for him; in one sense it was always one-sided. She goes on, all through her life, insisting this relationship is the most important thing, that they are primarily a couple, and that's impressive and moving. But as I re-read the autobiographies I started to ask more questions. In one way the relationship with Sartre is absolutely the centre of her life and books, but in another it is an extraordinary absence. There are so many things that she doesn't write about; she does shy away from talking about the sexual side of the relationship, and from negative feelings like jealousy. She admits she is disturbed by Olga, and by a later friend of Sartre, whom she calls M.; she wonders if his relationship with them isn't deeper than with her. But she manages to dismiss all that. They do survive as a couple; but we're left asking, 'What kind of couple?' What does that all-important word mean?

Particularly as they got older, I think there are hints of alienation and unhappiness. On one level she presents a rosy picture with a kind of gallant determination, but at the same time she is a good enough writer and honest enough to be constantly querying.

She wrote *Adieux* when Sartre was very ill. It's a terrifying book, because it's an extraordinarily detailed record of his illness and senility and helplessness and pain; as she had done all through her life, she records his doings in the most meticulous and tiny detail. That in itself must have been very difficult. But it was also a period when she and Sartre were for various reasons increasingly alienated from each other, and so her attempt to write this book and to record conversations with him is a way of insisting, 'No, this relationship is still the most important thing in my life and his life as well.' I find it very disturbing to read, because it expresses not just grief and fear and horror about illness and old age, but anger as well. The detail with which she records his pain and symptoms occasionally takes on a slightly sadistic tinge. Her anger breaks through – at the ravages of old age, but also at a Sartre who even on his death-bed somehow eludes her.

She started getting interested in old age remarkably young. She was hardly middle-aged when she first talked about her fear and hatred of old age. She then went on to write a fascinating book about old age, as well as writing in great detail about her mother's death and about Sartre dying. I think it's partly because age is the ultimate challenge. All her life Simone de Beauvoir in a sense lived in the future; but that future inevitably contracts and disappears.

Childhood is never important for her on its own terms – it's simply an apprenticeship to the future, to the adult world. Her whole life is projected into the future; she sees being human as transcending nature. Well, in old age, nature wins. It cannot be transcended, it's the final challenge to her kind of rational and optimistic philosophy. I think that's one of the reasons she returns to it again and again. It also brings out some of her finest writing – I think one of the most moving things she ever wrote was the book about her mother called, ironically, *A Very Easy Death*. It's moving because for the first time she has to confront things that she can't even begin to control, and she finds herself identifying with her mother in all sorts of ways.

She makes careful, meticulous notes on what is happening – that is always one of her ways of controlling a situation: ordering it, making it possible to live through it – but at the same time she finds herself a helpless child with her mother dying. She sees in her mother what her own old age and death are going to be like. There's one very powerful moment when she realizes that she is actually looking like her mother, her mouth is moving in the way that her mother's mouth did. She is brought up against something that she can't – none of us can – control.

> When my father died I did not cry at all. I said to my sister, 'It will be the same for Maman.' I had understood all my sorrows until that night: even when they flowed over my head I recognized myself in them. This time my despair escaped from my control: someone other than myself was weeping in me. I talked to Sartre about my mother's mouth as I had seen it – greediness refused, an almost servile humility, hope, distress, loneliness – the loneliness of her death and of her life – that did not want to admit its **49**

existence. And he told me that my own mouth was not obeying me any more: I had put Maman's mouth on my own face and in spite of myself, I copied its movements. Her whole person, her whole being, was concentrated there, and compassion wrung my heart.

from *A Very Easy Death*

I think that some of her power comes from the way she acknowledges, out of the corner of her eye, areas of confusion. One of the things that makes her books exciting to read, the novels as well as the autobiography, is the clarity of the structure – they are always enormously optimistic, patterned. She has written in some ways to prove a thesis. The autobiographies are proving that it is possible to escape from conventional femininity, from oppression, to achieve genuine freedom. And each of the novels in its way, I think, has got a philosophical thesis. But the real power lies in her rational clarity coming up against the shadows, then she touches on everything that's confused and non-rational – childhood, sexuality, death.

I met her once, briefly, in the mid-seventies when she was beginning to get very interested in the new women's movement. I went with a friend to her flat in Paris to interview her. She was very impressive and certainly formidable, tremendously articulate, talking non-stop and it was quite hard to get a question in edgeways. Like her books, she was full of paradoxes. You had the sense of a person who had made up her mind, who had her opinions, and you were going to bounce off that fairly armour-plated exterior. But at the same time she was much prettier than I had expected. She was a very feminine-looking woman, and in her flat the whole atmosphere was remarkably cosy and domesticated. She was charming, conventionally pretty, she was quite girlish – there was something very engaging about her and about the flat, which was full of dolls and souvenirs. She seemed an extremely complicated woman, just from that one glimpse of her.

I think she is a very important writer, in some ways more so than Sartre though she would not agree. One of the paradoxes of her life is that she tended to put Sartre first, always insisting that he was the more ideologically creative, that he always took the philosophical and political initiative. That was true up to a point, but Sartre was writing very much within a familiar philosophical and political tradition, and she was doing something really new. I don't think that any one of her books, standing alone, is necessarily great, but I do think the body of the work over a lifetime added up to something genuinely original and important. Not just the fact that she had the confidence to use her own life in the way she did (something that not very many women have had the confidence to do), but also the fact that she used her own life to explore her intellectual preoccupations. I remember one French critic a few years ago who called it the most important feminist project ever undertaken, the whole of her life's work – and I agree with that.

Angie Pegg

5
Angie Pegg

I was brought up in Malawi, which used to be called Nyasaland, and I was the third of four children. My father was born there; his father had gone out to Africa after the First World War. I grew up as a colonial Catholic child. It was a very strict upbringing. I went to a Catholic boarding school run by nuns when I was ten, and spent two or three years in abject misery. I hated it. I was very religious but also quite rebellious, always getting into trouble. I was very angry and didn't work, and was quite disaffected – yet I used to go on retreats and promise God that I would be good, and then be 'naughty' within five minutes.

We lived in Malawi until I was sixteen, when we came to England, and lived in Colchester. I moved to Nottingham with a boyfriend when I was twenty-one. I thought I was quite old and sophisticated when I got married, I was almost twenty-three. I had a very quick, intense romance – a friend of mine became very ill, so I came down from Nottingham to Colchester to look after her and her little boy. It turned out that she had cancer, and I looked after her son for a few months while she was in hospital, and met and fell in love with my first husband at the same time. It was a very intense time because my friend was dying, but also because I was falling in love. I used to feel guilty because I was falling in love and she was slipping away. When her little boy was taken away to be adopted after she died, I felt I wanted to have my own child, and I chose my first husband really to have a child with.

We got married in November 1973 and I had a child eleven months later. Our first wedding anniversary was accompanied by the strains of a screaming baby, who didn't do much else but cry.

Part of the reason I wanted to get married to my husband was that he had a lot that was feminine about him: he was gentle, he had long hair (but everybody did then), he was very artistic and musical and I felt very empathetic to him in lots of ways. But when I had this boy, this son, I remember walking in from the ambulance, coming home with my child, he rushed out of the door and said, 'I've got to go to work.' It was very significant, because he felt that because he had a son – particularly a son, I think – he had to go out there and work, and he never came back, in a way. We had had a marvellous time with the honeymoon and the pregnancy and everything, then as soon as Tom was born he felt that he had to bring home the bacon. He was self-employed and so he was away all the time. It didn't start too well, really.

I had another child nearly four years later, but actually we were very happy then; my husband had had a very bad accident but survived, and we had another chance. While he was at home I conceived our second child, after trying for quite a long time to have another one. It was good because it was a new start for us, we were very happy, the birth was good and everything was different and much easier. But after that, things began going downhill. I got very depressed after the second one.

I thought I was all right and I expected to be a bit tearful, because I had been with the first one. My image of myself became quite negative and distorted. We were living in a small town in Essex, and I remember going out every day and going a different way to the shops just to experience something different. I used to go three or four miles out of my way to go to the Co-op. But one day I felt very strange. I had had experiences of being detached from my body, anxiety, my heart would flutter quite a lot. I went into a fruit shop – I had my eldest child with me who was about four, and the young child in the pushchair – I looked at the fruit and I didn't know what it was. I had a moment of real panic, I had this money in my hand and I didn't know what the money was. I felt very weird. I looked at Dan's head in the pushchair and that was the only thing that connected me to anything.

I managed to get home, although I don't remember much about it. I must have been on automatic, as a parent you just have to cope. I rang a friend, I don't even remember ringing her, and she came round and I just sort of collapsed. I didn't feel real. I kept saying to her, 'Talk to me, talk to me,' so that I could feel real. After that I only went out about twice, quickly to the shops and then back. I stayed at home for about three weeks before I went to the doctor. It was very painful and I didn't know what was wrong. I thought I was mad.

I began looking for answers to what was wrong with me, because although I thought I was probably mad, I thought I had a private individual problem. I knew from reading *Woman's Own* - I used to read the problem pages avidly in the doctor's surgery, because even then I wouldn't buy magazines like that, I thought they were daft. People would say things like, 'I don't fancy making love to my husband any more, what is wrong with me?' And the answer would always be, 'Oh, come on dear, get a nice sexy nightie and everything will be all right.' So I never found any compensation in that.

I saw Simone de Beauvoir's book one day in the bookshop and I just bought it because it was called *The Second Sex* and that was intriguing. I read the bit about housework. I bought it one day in 1979 and I started reading it about eight o'clock and I don't think I went to bed until four, it just turned me inside out. It was as if somebody had come into the room and talked to me for the first time, and said, 'It's all right to feel what you are feeling. It's all right.' And what was so amazing was that other women felt it as well, thousands and millions of them. For the first time in my life somebody actually validated what I was feeling and said, 'Yes, it's not because you are mad or bad.'

I was very uncritical, of course. I could read it now and think, God I don't agree with this, that and the other: the way she uses 'he' all the time, for instance, but that's not what is really important. What is important was that somebody actually said, 'It's all right to feel what you are feeling, it's understandable. In fact you have every reason to feel how you feel.' When I read the bit about housework I found it most astonishing. I used to cook slavishly for hours every day, and I used to stuff the children with food. I am a very good cook and I enjoyed it, but there was something driving me. I felt I was a slave to it. I used to produce these wonderful things and go out and get all the raw materials, I would never buy anything that was packet or frozen. I would produce this wonderful meal and they would scoff it in about two minutes. I used to sit there and almost feel like crying - well, sometimes I did. I would feel dismay and yet I felt confused because I was supposed to feel good. On the one hand, on the surface, I used to think, 'Oh, good, they are going to be alive for another day, strong and healthy, strapping lads, they are alive because of me,' and that justified my existence. But at the same time I felt, 'Bloody hell, I have done all this and they've scoffed it, and it's gone, it's destroyed.' My husband was a tree surgeon, he would cut trees down and they would be there lying on the ground, but everything I did just disappeared for ever.

> 'Washing, ironing, sweeping, ferreting out fluff from under wardrobes – all this halting of decay is also a denial of life, for time simultaneously creates and destroys . . . A continual renunciation is required of the woman whose operations are completed only in their destruction.'

from *The Second Sex*

There was some compensation of course, seeing the boys grow up, but the more they grew the less I grew, the more shrunken I became. Reading de Beauvoir made me realize how real it is that men exist in the outside public domain, they are citizens, and we live our lives through them.

> 'She perpetuates the species without change . . . but she is allowed no direct influence upon the future nor upon the world; she reaches out beyond herself towards the social group only through her husband as intermediary.'

from *The Second Sex*

My husband would come home and I used to say to him almost hungrily, 'What's it like out there, what's going on out there?' At the times when I became very distraught, like in the fruit shop, it was because it was 'out there' and my whole reality was based only at home, my connections with the outside world were only through him.

> 'the home becomes the centre of the world and even its only reality; . . . refuge, retreat, grotto, womb . . . it is the confused outer world that becomes unreal. Reality is concentrated inside the house, while outer space seems to *collapse* (my emphasis).

from *The Second Sex*

56   She said all that, you see, it was amazing. It wasn't as if she had invented it, it was as if it had always been like that but I hadn't been able to put all the pieces together. I don't think it would have meant so much to me if I hadn't thought about it a lot already, but she pulled it all together for me.

I began to challenge my situation and that's where the trouble started. There's a bit in *The Second Sex* where she says, 'on the one hand you are constantly claiming your independence and defying him but on the other hand you are constantly trying to maintain your dependence.' I was frightened because although I was middle-class, I didn't have any money or anything, and also my husband was very handsome and lots of people liked him. People used to say to me, 'You'll never get another one like him.' It was terribly important to have a good-looking, nice bloke because at that time it was unimaginable to be without one. When we got married I sort of gave him my identity and said, 'Here, you look after this, make sure you look after it OK'. After reading de Beauvoir and other things, it was as if I was saying, 'Well, I'll have that bit back, and that bit back . . .' And he resisted it. I don't think it was his fault. I think I punished him for all the anger at my life, at being a girl and being told I couldn't do maths and leaving school with no 'O' levels. My anger rained down on him, and that wasn't fair.

A few months after reading de Beauvoir, I realized I had to do something for myself. I had been on anti-depressants and had gone up to Tom's school like a zombie. I just thought, 'Christ, I can't handle this, this is like death.' I remember pushing the pushchair up this long hill one day thinking, 'This is *it*. This is all there is.' I used to watch people going to work with this sort of amazement, feeling like a slave, and thinking (I know it sounds corny), 'I'll never have the chance to be like them.'

I applied to university with quite a lot of resistance on the part of my husband, because he felt very strongly that Dan, who was only two and a half, should be looked after by me. I think that made me feel very guilty, but I applied, and got in. I walked into the interview and it was incredible – I told them that they should really have me there. That was the first time I had been confident for a long time. I was very frightened, but I was so determined to go. I started feeling very guilty, but nevertheless I went. Dan went to nursery and Tom went to school and then I began the juggling act that all women have: who picks up who; sitting in a philosophy lecture thinking about fish fingers – all   **57** those problems. And then thinking, 'Why should I do all the housework, I'm going to work every day.' It just disintegrated from there. My husband didn't like my studying. I think he was prepared to put up with it as long as it didn't interfere with what he considered to be 'real life'.

De Beauvoir gave me some insight into the fact that my husband's identity and his reality were actually 'out there'. I used to think privately that when he came home, that was the real him and I was the only one with access to it. But in fact I think she's right, I think he *did* exist more as himself in his social identity and that's what is so terrible about staying at home: you don't have any social identity. You are literally not a social being. That's why I went to university. I think that learning is a social experience – I could have done the Open University, but I wanted to be with people.

I did philosophy because I wanted answers. I did it partly because Simone de Beauvoir was a philosopher and because I thought she was probably better than Sartre, but when I got there, of course I studied Sartre and Freud and the great patriarchs. Simone de Beauvoir was nowhere to be seen, in fact there was only one of her books in the library. But all the theoretical work I did at university was formed by people like de Beauvoir, by my experience of being at home, and my upbringing. I began to think very carefully about subjective experience and knowledge, and that was very much resisted by male lecturers. I met resistance at university on the same scale as I had at home. Although it was different and more sophisticated, I believe now that it had the same basis, in that women just don't count, whether they are at home or whether they are writers or philosophers.

I studied Sartre and what he said about sex, and I began to realize a lot about de Beauvoir being Sartre's mother, a lot about the male being the subject. But my own experience at home was really what informed my studying and it has taught me more about the world than my three years at university. I am a teacher now and I'm always trying to make connections between these things. I feel that if any student came to see me at home they wouldn't find an essentially different person, and that is all to do with what de Beauvoir was saying about how we divide ourselves up between the private and the public domain.

I had an individualized, private problem. I went to the

doctor and got valium and anti-depressants, and then I read de Beauvoir and started to realize the whole experience was a social one, there were reasons for it and other women experienced it. That was very important. It transformed my entire life.

I went to university with a lot of mature students and they started having problems. A lot of them were women, women returning. One of the first things that happens to everybody is you have to get home late one night, so you get your husband to come home early and you have to try and renegotiate or contract different household jobs. When you've been doing all the housework yourself for a long time, it's a big change. I used to feel that unless you were really supported domestically, then you couldn't really do it – and I wasn't. In fact I remember a time when my husband used to stay out even longer, on purpose. I think it was hard for him as well and I have some sympathy for him, because one minute this woman is marrying you and saying she wants lots of babies and she wants to be yours for ever, and the next . . . It is a bit hard, and I think we tended to entrench our two positions. If I had to do an essay I would do everything at home, then stay up till three or four in the morning and go in exhausted next day. But every now and then I thought, 'Damn, why should I?' We just ended up rowing all the time. It was very difficult because I wanted his support in a very concrete, practical way – I didn't want a pat on the back. I thought then and I still think now that until men look after children as well, the world isn't going to change enough.

Simone de Beauvoir always talked about having children as if it was a disgusting thing. In *The Second Sex* she goes on and on about domesticity and housework and how awful it is, and she says, 'and if you've got young children to look after as well . . .!' But I would disagree with her on that, because I think having children has taught me almost everything I know. It forces you to really look at who you are.

I remember watching Dan in a high chair aged five or six months, dropping a rattle and me picking it up and putting it back in his hand, and all of a sudden he looked at the rattle and threw it again, realizing at that moment that he was a separate entity. Things like that are a powerful indication of separate identity, and they taught me a lot, philosophically in a sense. I am always reluctant to separate theory from practice, and I

top
Angie Pegg as a baby in her
mother's arms

middle
Angie (far right) at her
first communion, in
Nyasaland

bottom
As a teenager, with her horse

opposite page (top)
Angie with her baby son
during her first marriage

bottom
With her first husband and
two sons

top
Angie on graduation day with
her two sons

bottom
With her second husband and
three children

think that if she had had that kind of experience she would have been enriched by it. But I also suspect that she didn't have children because she didn't want to spoil that special relationship with Sartre. When you have kids they often do occupy the space between you, and they do put stress on your relationship. She probably knew that. I admire women who choose not to have children, in a way. I don't think there's anything wrong with her not wanting children, I just never felt the same as she did.

I think she was probably a little enslaved by Sartre. I think of her as Sartre's 'other', although I respect her tremendously and I think she was probably much more wonderful, and in fact historically I think she will endure much longer than him. Already nobody reads *Being and Nothingness* any more; his books were all right, but they were a bit wacky. I think he had a lot of power over her, and that comes through in a lot of her writing.

I thought about her in relation to him sexually, and I didn't feel she was there at all when he was talking about sex. In his writing it's all very abstract and very male and quite brutal in some ways. He doesn't have the gentleness that she has about things, or the understanding. It's all about performance and not feelings.

In a way, she was a motherly role for me – perhaps more like an elder sister, the elder sister that I would have liked to have had. But there's something very liberating about thinking of her as a motherly figure, because she said the sort of things that I wanted my mother to say to me. For instance, when I told my mother I was going to university, the first thing she said was, 'What about your husband and children?' What she meant was that they should come first. I was very angry and dismayed at that, whereas I had this fantasy of ringing Simone de Beauvoir up and she would say, 'Great, great, go for it, what are you going to study? Just give me a ring if you need any help.' She was really there.

My mother and I, were all tied up in being mothers, you see, and that's what Simone de Beauvoir talks about – the isolation of being at home. It's hard to be really good friends with your kids if you have to be their mother all day. I think she knew all those things. I used to wonder how she knew them, but she did – I don't think you have to have kids to know things like that.

Now I'm with another partner and I've got a daughter, which was wonderful for me, and I'm very glad I didn't have one before, because I would have decked her out in pink from top to bottom! I've sorted out the sort of woman I think I am, or want to be, whereas when I had the boys I didn't really know who I was. It's completely different, and it's wonderful. If you know something about who you are, you can't neurotically live through your children, and having a daughter has been very exciting because I like myself now, and I didn't then. I feel I have a right to all these feelings and I understand more about myself. I'm very proud to have given birth to someone who is going to be a woman, who can be strong, and is not going to hear the things that I heard about myself all her life.

The only thing that I find negative about the experience is the way other people treat her. I hear echoes of my past, like people saying 'Isn't she pretty?' and 'She won't ever have to be very clever, will she?' Yes, it has been a positive experience. Things are changing and I go to work now, so when I see her it is real 'quality time' and not just endless hours and hours of playing with Lego and reading the same books, which I hated.

When Dan went to school I threw out all the books – I think I knew I was going to have another baby, and I wanted to do it right, you see. But I don't really think there is a 'right' way, I'm not looking for answers any more. I came out at the end of university knowing there aren't any, and it was very liberating. I know now there isn't a right way of being a mother, and I go to work feeling that she has the best time with me. I really wish the boys had had it.

Also her father is very involved. When she was born, I went out to work a few weeks afterwards, doing part-time lecturing, and he stayed at home for a year and found that terribly rewarding and frustrating, but a very important experience. He looks after her now because he's a student at university, and I'm at work and I come in quite late, at six or seven sometimes, but when I walk in the door, I look around and I *know* how much labour has gone into the whole situation. I know what it has taken for him to cook a meal, to look after Katy, to manage the boys – pick them up from whatever they've been doing. I don't think a lot of women have that. Men don't walk into a house and know what is involved. I know I support him in a way that I was never supported, because I will never treat anyone the way I was treated. That doesn't mean to say it's all perfect – sometimes I wish I was at home, and I think: 'no brain, no pain'. If only I could just go to school every day and pick them up, just be ordinary. But you can't, when you've been through all that. I really enjoy work and feel enriched by it and enjoy my children a lot more now. My relationship with my partner now is different – I'm a lot more independent, and it's just much easier. I do believe, though, that relationships between women and men are always going to be unequal so long as we have a society that treats women as secondary, as 'other'. I think that for any woman, a relationship with a man must involve compromise and contradiction. It just depends how much you're prepared to accept. Like de Beauvoir, I think there is still something deeply conventional in me, which conflicts with my experience of sexism in the world. Nevertheless, my life is much better now than I could have imagined ten years ago.

I never used to go on holiday much with my first husband and the boys. He used to say, 'Let's go away,' and I used to think, 'By the time I've got into the car . . .', because I had to pack and think about bottles and antiseptic cream and leaving a note for the milkman; I had to do every bloody thing. By the time I got in the car I'd be flaked out and miserable, but now I don't have that burden and so we go on holiday. We've both done it, and we've both got energy. I think that's what it's all about, having energy.

Ann Oakley

6
Ann Oakley

My father was an academic, he had a professorship at a university, and my mother stayed at home. I went to a girls' direct-grant school from the age of six to sixteen, when I walked out, thinking that this was not what education was supposed to be about.

I went to a poly and did my A levels. I had a wonderful time, and discovered that the world contained two sexes, something that until then I hadn't been aware of. Then I went to Oxford and did a Social Science degree, unlike my father, who had come from quite an impoverished family, and he had gone out to work at fourteen to support his brother and sister. I had a much more privileged background in comparison, but I was a different sex from him and I had this problem of the contradictions between the two roles, which we all still have.

My copy of *The Second Sex* was given to me by my first boyfriend in 1960. He wrote in it something like, 'To Ann from Christopher, with love.' I didn't understand at the time quite why he gave it to me. I didn't read it then, but I've read it since, as you can tell because it's now falling apart and held together with an elastic band.

I have trouble remembering when I started to read it, but it must have been in the late sixties. I had two small children, I was trying to adjust to the role of full-time mother, and not succeeding very well. I decided to register for a PhD and to study the attitudes of women to housework, to look at the housework side of motherhood as a job. In order to do that, I found myself reading an enormous amount of literature, because that sort of question leads you to ask really basic questions about why the roles of men and women are different. In the course of pursuing those questions I read *The Second Sex*.

I found it really inspiring, in common with many other people – many other women. I think it was because of the very strong statement that it contained, that these things are nothing **67** to do with biology, they are not determined for you except by social forces. Therefore, there was room for change. That was a really inspiring message. Also de Beauvoir covers an enormous number of areas in that book – she covers anthropology, economics, psychology, psychoanalysis – a whole range of disciplines; that, too, was inspiring.

There was nothing else that did what *The Second Sex* did in terms of analysing why women are in the state they are in, or of the areas and disciplines that were covered in coming to those conclusions. The nearest contender was Betty Friedan's *The Feminine Mystique*, which, for me, was a book largely about American culture, whereas I think de Beauvoir's is much more universal in its appeal and coverage.

In some ways *The Second Sex* stands the test of time well, in some ways it doesn't. It's been criticized for being a very white, middle-class account of the situation of women, and I think that's true. De Beauvoir's analysis of marriage, for instance, is restricted to the circles from which she came, and I think people, even people in England, have had some difficulties with that kind of presentation.

There are limiting aspects to it, but I think in terms of the breadth of analysis it offers it still has the ability to inspire. It's a book that to me seems to have been written with passion, and the passion still comes through; we need that passion still, perhaps we need it more in 1989 than we did twenty years ago.

My taking on the subject of housework as a PhD subject was regarded as a huge joke by the male academic establishment at the time, who thought that I must be thinking about something quite different. Various attempts were made to make me study the sexual satisfaction of women in marriage, that being the nearest they could get to seeing there was actually something serious to be studied in the role of women in the home, so it was with great difficulty that I found a supervisor and struggled through the process of doing a PhD.

Simone de Beauvoir never had children, of course, and she said once that she never regretted not having children because mother–daughter relationships were so awful. She assumed, I suppose, that if she was going to have children she would have had female children, which might not have been the case! However, I think she felt very ambivalent about her own mother and that comes out in a lot of what she wrote. Almost because she didn't have children herself, I think she didn't come to experience the positive side in the next generation, and that has been the criticism levelled at her work by a lot of people, i.e. by rejecting motherhood, she cut herself off from a whole area of women's experience and therefore was unable to say anything about it. I think to some extent that's true.

For me, though, motherhood has been the most enjoyable and the most difficult thing I've ever done. It's a constant challenge. I have one son and two daughters and it's different according to the sex of the child and according to your own age and what you were doing at the time, and so on. It has been and still is very important to me. There are moments when I realize life is limited, and at those times I realize that it's the one thing I'm glad I've done. There's a gap between what I feel about the position of women, in relation to my experience, and to what de Beauvoir said.

I think it's quite common for women to want to do it differently from their own mothers, to feel very confident at the beginning that they *can* do it differently – and then what happens is that you hear yourself talking to your children one day, and you hear your mother! The tone of voice is the same, the sentiments are the same, and you think, 'Where did that come from?' It's an extremely powerful experience, but having said that, I think the message of *The Second Sex*, or the message of a lot of feminist writing, is that if only we can understand why we are doing things and why we are saying things, then we can change. I think you *can* change, and I think that on the whole this generation of mothers and daughters is able to discuss things more openly, including the ambivalences and the negative side of parenting. I think it's easier than it has been, but what the daughters will do in their turn I have no idea.

I can't wait to be a grandmother. People always say that that relationship gives you the positive side without the negative side. Well, we'll see, it may never happen.

Simone de Beauvoir has been a very important role model for me, as she has been for lots of other women, and in that sense she has been a mother, the mother some of us perhaps wished we had ourselves. Like one's own mother, I think we thought of her as being immortal, so that the news of her death, when it came, **69**

above left Ann Oakley as a baby with her father, Professor Richard Titmuss

above right Ann as a child

below As a teenager with the boyfriend who gave her a copy of *The Second Sex*

left
Ann on graduation day,
with her husband

centre
With two of her children as
babies

bottom
With her family in the 1970s

Ann in 1988

was very shocking – it simply hadn't occurred to us that there would be a world that didn't contain her.

Both her writing and her life were important to us in terms of presenting a model, not necessarily one that we follow directly. I think the idea of an independent woman was an ideal that she never achieved, which it is perhaps impossible to achieve and perhaps not a very good thing to achieve, but she was at least struggling for it. I think a lot of her own autobiography is an attempt to present a rational view of her life – to make it into a project without contradictions, in which she does achieve this aim of being independent. Perhaps it is as much the contradictions that we identify with, because we feel them and we live through them, and we can't find a solution either.

She has admitted there are things she doesn't talk about in her autobiography, for instance she found it difficult to be open and honest about her sexuality. Perhaps she was the wrong generation for that, it's one of the areas in which her background comes out. The influence of her mother, who didn't think these things were proper and didn't talk about them, was something that she couldn't change. There were some things which she could and other things which she couldn't change, and I'm sure there's a great deal about her relationship with Sartre that she doesn't discuss, too. The nearest she comes to some of that is in *Adieux*, the book in which she interviews Sartre – that's the way she did it, she interviewed him about their relationship and that enabled her to reveal some aspects of it that she couldn't write about directly.

I think it comes over quite strongly in *Adieux* that she regards Sartre as possessing a superior knowledge about most things, including about her, and about their relationship. It also comes out in the rest of her writings and some of the things she said very early on about the influence that led her to write certain things. She didn't believe being a woman made any difference in her life until he told her that it did, and then she sat down and started to write *The Second Sex*. She wasn't a feminist when she published it, but when she got reactions from women – 'You are writing about me, you are writing about us' – then she became a feminist. So his role as the person who possessed superior wisdom in her life was incredibly important. In that sense her idea of being an independent woman – her ideal of

73

being free within a relationship – simply was not matched by reality. And that's quite reassuring to many women who can't do it either.

If she had done it all perfectly – if she had found the ultimate solution in maintaining a completely equal relationship – then she wouldn't have been real as a role model, as a mother. It's because she *didn't* solve these problems, although she wrote endlessly and beautifully about them, with great insight. Yet in her own life the struggle continued. I don't think it is inevitable, the fact that women tend to get involved in these kinds of relationships, but it does happen quite a lot, and it obviously is a reflection of all kinds of deep-seated notions about female and male socialization, and all those other things.

When I wrote my own autobiography I learned the important lesson from her that there is a great deal you *don't* write about, and that you can create the appearance of a revelation but actually keep a whole lot of important things hidden. When I read the volumes of her autobiography, I was left feeling that I didn't really know her, there was a lot she hadn't written about. The overall impression was that this was the way she wished to see her life. If she could have constructed it, this was how she would have constructed it. But on the emotional level and in terms of how she felt in everyday life, I don't think that came through.

Everyone who has ever written an autobiography must know that you can't reveal a great number of things. You make the choices of what to leave out partly on the basis of not wishing to upset or involve people who are still alive – that is the problem about writing an autobiography in middle-age, which she and I did; and you make them partly on the basis of what is just too painful to write about at the time. There is another thing, too, that I knew before I wrote my own autobiography, which came out of her experience of writing something of hers. That is the importance to other women of what you are doing and the responses you get when you publish the book. It doesn't feel like a personal project, it feels like something which is more public, more important.

I had lots and lots of letters from women, many of whom wrote at great length about their own lives and ended by saying, 'I'm sorry I've written this, but I felt I had to send it.' Of course I don't hear from the people who don't want to write letters having read it, so it's a very selective audience that I get to hear about, but it still is extremely important to know that the themes one has written about are of general interest.

My father was a very gentle person – my feeling as a child was of my mother being the 'strong one' – but my father was the person who had a role in the public domain, with success and achievement, in terms of conventional male values about what achievement is. It's terribly common for women who essentially do the male thing, as it could be argued women like de Beauvoir and myself did, to have fathers like that. It has been pointed out that all the female prime ministers so far have had exactly this kind of pattern – they didn't have any brothers, they had mothers who were at home and they had fathers who pushed them and who were successful. That's quite problematic, it's problematic in relation to the mother, because if the father is that important then what does it say about the role of the mother? I don't think de Beauvoir really got around to working out the answer to that one.

The book she wrote about her mother dying, *A Very Easy Death*, is interesting on this. There's a point where she said her mother was very proud of her, but disapproved of everything she had done, and I think that puts it very nicely. I think lots of people have exactly that feeling, in that there is a great gulf of understanding, but the wish to be pleased with one's daughter is very strong.

> Why did my mother's death shake me so deeply? Since the time I left home I had felt little in the way of emotional impulse towards her . . . Generally speaking I thought of her with no particular feeling. Yet in my sleep (although my father only made very rare and then insignificant appearances) she often played a most important part: she blended with Sartre, and we were happy together. And then the dream would turn into a nightmare: why was I living with her once more? How had I come to be in her power again? So our former relationship lived on in me in its double aspect – a subjection that I loved and hated . . .
>
> There are photographs of both of us, taken at about the same time: I am eighteen, she is nearly forty. Today I could almost be her mother and the grandmother of that

sad-eyed girl. I am so sorry for them – for me because I am so young and I understand nothing; for her because her future is closed and she has never understood anything. But I would not know how to advise them. It was not in my power to wipe out the unhappinesses in her childhood that condemned Maman to make me unhappy and to suffer in her turn from having done so. For if she embittered several years of my life, I certainly paid her back though I did not set out to do so.

from *A Very Easy Death*

Marta Zabaleta Hinrichsen

7
Marta Zabaleta Hinrichsen

I was brought up in Argentina, in the countryside, in an area called Santa Fé. I was the only child of a middle-class family, but both my parents were workers really – my mother was a primary school teacher and my father was a civil servant. I grew up in a very strict family.

My mother saw a review of one of Simone de Beauvoir's books in a newspaper, and she told me, 'It seems to me that this woman is going to understand you better than I do, so I'll get this book for you as a present.' I was twenty-two. She gave me the book, but as it was given to me by her, I thought, 'Well, she doesn't understand anything about adolescents,' and so I didn't read it. Then we went away on holiday, and when we came back my mother suddenly died, very soon after. I thought, 'Perhaps I will find some consolation in that book she gave me.' I started to read the book, it was called *Memoirs of a Dutiful Daughter*. And that's how I came across the first book of Simone de Beauvoir that I read. It was 1960.

I thought it was marvellous, very well-written, but I particularly liked the way in which she confronted the conflicts of a woman coming from a middle-class background, with all the problems and misunderstandings of the father and the family about her hopes and aspirations. It made me feel really comfortable to read about a person having the same problems as me – there weren't really a lot of similarities in our situations, but in my mind my life looked like hers. I was very touched by what she said about her relationships with her male colleagues and friends; it was very impressive because I was at university at that time, and I tended to have much closer relationships with boys than with girls.

Ordinarily, a girl of my age in Argentina would have been married and looking forward to having at least two or three children. The usual way you could work would be in so-called 'feminine activities', like primary education, nursing or some thing like that. About 20 per cent of the workforce as a whole were women, not a lot really. So you would look after your house, your husband, your parents and your parents-in-law as well. The family was at the centre of all activities. Divorce was beginning to become acceptable, but divorce was considered something extremely wrong in my family, so no one talked about it; there was no divorce in the whole family. You were expected to be a very conventional woman, interested in feminine, pretty things, if possible thinking all the time about clothes, talking about women's things, visiting your friends, playing cards, this sort of thing.

I thought it was a pity that all my friends were getting married, and I tried to change their minds, because most of them were very young. Some of them started to work as primary teachers as well, but the richer ones tended to stay at home, with one or two domestic servants. Most of them were quite able – I knew them very well because they had been my friends from secondary school. I thought it was a pity, but I helped them with their duties because I was very fond of my friends. I failed totally in making even one of them study for a degree.

Immediately after I read *Memoirs of a Dutiful Daughter* I began to read the second book of her memoirs, and I found it much more interesting than the previous one because it was written around the Second World War and the Resistance. Also she was starting her career in teaching, and her relationship with Sartre became much deeper and more intense. I was impressed by what she said about a woman pursuing a career. She said it was better for women not to marry or have children, because of the complications motherhood and especially marriage would bring to their careers. I took this very seriously and I thought that if I was going to fulfil myself professionally, it would be much better to be single than to get married.

This was very much against my mother's wishes. She always complained that I would be alone, lonely all my life and no one would take care of me. When I was seventeen my mother was really afraid that I would be single all my life. The word in Argentina for women who don't marry is *solterona*. She called me a *solterona* from when I was seventeen: 'Marta is a *solterona*.' You know, it was quite hurtful. You look upon yourself as normal, even when you're not normal according to the standard of the country.

I suspect that in Buenos Aires it would have been possible to develop a more normal life for a person of my age, but we were living in a place which wasn't exactly in the countryside, but it was a small town, San Nicolás. Everyone knew each other and gossiped all the time. Being married and having children is a sign of status, and if you hadn't got that, you were considered a failure by all the family, no matter what else you did. If you went to university, it was viewed as a sort of disaster, despite the fact that Argentinian women have been going to university for a century – the first woman doctor got her degree at the end of the last century. In spite of all that, the people had no use for it. They were resentful because they saw you as an independent person.

The Prime of Life was very important to me; it gave me encouragement. After I read it I actually wrote to her. There were some things I wanted to discuss with her personally, as I didn't know any other women who thought like I did.

I didn't know how to get in touch with her, of course, so I went to the French Consulate in Rosario, knocked at the door, and asked the man who answered if he could help me to find the address of this French author, Simone de Beauvoir. He said he didn't know what I was talking about, and I was a little shocked. I told myself, 'Well, don't give up', and asked him if he knew the address of Jean-Paul Sartre. He said, 'No, how on earth would I know that?' I said, 'Could you find it out for me? He is a very famous writer.' The man said, 'Yes, I think I've heard his name before.' A fortnight later, he came round to my house and he had got the address. I was delighted, and wrote to Jean-Paul in Spanish saying that I was a young person very interested in his books, but although I liked his books very much, I liked Simone de Beauvoir's better, so I wanted to get in touch with her to discuss my personal problems and to let her know that her books have had enormous influence on people's lives, that she ought to keep going, and keep writing. I asked him if he would do me the favour of asking her to write back to me.

Several months later, I received a letter from Simone telling me that she was quite pleased, quite touched by my letter, very pleased that it had got to her hands finally. She had given a lot of thought to what I said, and these things encouraged her to keep writing her memoirs. I wrote back to her immediately, and after a while she replied to me again. I was questioning some of her ideas at the time, because there were things I was not clear about. I wanted to hear her opinion, if she was critical of herself at that stage. I also wrote to her about what was the best thing for me to do in my life, if I should be an economist or a writer and philosopher and come to live in Paris.

She advised me to go to Paris and she said she would help me if I needed any help. I ought to be courageous and break with my situation altogether, because she thought that I was not very happy. She said they would help me to find a place to live, and she thought I would not have any problems – strangely enough, she never mentioned the fact that I wrote in Spanish.

I couldn't follow her advice, in fact, because my father was horrified at the whole business of me having a so-called friend abroad, a woman who was not married, had no children, who said it was all wrong to be married and who gave women all these strange ideas. I was a socialist and a feminist. He was horrified, quite sad really, and angry as well. We were living together because my mother had died and I was looking after him, despite the fact that he was a very healthy person. You have to look after men in Argentina.

It made a huge impression on me, very discouraging. He said that I would be lost, I would become a prostitute, I would lose my career, I wouldn't earn any money, and I would come back a total failure, with nothing, having ruined my life. His opinion was very important to me at the time. There was a decision to be made between being a career woman in the traditional sense of being an accountant with an office and clients; or being totally free and doing what I really wanted to do, which was to write poems and novels. I wrote all the time, despite being an accountant. In my spare time I wrote poems and short stories and even a novel; I wanted to be a writer. Simone said I had the ability to be a writer, and that was very nice of her. I didn't manage to be a writer in the end, but I still hope to be one some day, because I think she was right, and I always regretted my decision.

After several months of thinking about what to do, the university suddenly decided to choose the best students of my generation to study abroad. Twelve of us were given a grant to go to the States or to Europe, where we would train as lecturers. I was very interested in seeing how the situation in our country could change, and for that purpose I thought I needed to

above
Marta Zabaleta as a baby

left
On holiday with her mother

below
With her father

opposite page
Marta (middle, front row) at university

With her husband, just before their marriage

above
Marta bending over her baby daughter, at the time of the Pinochet coup in Chile. The picture was taken so that her baby could be found if Marta were arrested. Marta has deliberately hidden her face

below
Marta's daughter and her husband, the day before he was imprisoned and became one of 'the disappeared' in Chile

understand more about economics and politics. I thought if I studied that systematically I could help my country. I was very impressed by Che Guevara then, by what he was doing in Cuba, and had done before in Guatemala and in other Latin American countries. He originally came from the same city as myself, Rosario, so I knew a lot about him. I chose to go to Chile in 1963 and for the first two years I studied for a Masters' degree in Santiago, but I kept in touch with the Chilean Society of Writers and kept on writing. When I finished my Masters', which was in Latin American Development Studies, I wrote to a woman who was a feminist and the chairperson of a huge organization belonging to the United Nations. I explained my situation to her, and said that now I was in a position to help women do things differently, so she gave me a job and I started to work at the United Nations in an official capacity. It was a very good job, very well paid. I started working on women's problems in Latin America, but she moved me to another job, we quarrelled over it, and finally I left. That was in 1965.

I had very strong views about marriage and children as a young woman. Changing my mind about them was a long process, but the main reason I began to think about them positively was the solitude I experienced in Southern Chile in a very conservative society, very primitive in comparison to where I had been living before. I felt very lonely. The other thing that made me think differently was that I began to notice how much I liked children. I began to think that having a career perhaps was not enough.

I married in 1969 because the army took over the university where I was a lecturer one morning, and I thought that otherwise I would be expelled from Chile. I was living with one of the school's students as my *compañero* and we decided to marry the following week because I naïvely thought that would make it all right. When the person marrying us had finished, I said to him, 'Well, now I'm a Chilean, aren't I?' He said, 'No, sorry, you're not. You have to apply for nationality.' That was the hardest thing, but nevertheless I was very happy because my boyfriend's family were worried about him living with me without being married. He was ten years younger than me, and his mother is a very conventional, conservative sort of person, even though she is very nice.

It helped, of course, that the man who is now my husband was a pleasant sort of person. He did not appear to be someone who would put pressure on my life. I had had proposals of marriage from other men, and because I always said, 'No, no, no,' apparently it became an attraction to them. This boy was different. He was younger, he belonged to a movement of socialist students in the south of Chile, a very famous movement of students. I was a foreigner, I was a woman and I was very young to be a lecturer according to the standards of the day, so I felt a social pressure to be married as well as it being an act of love.

When I grew older, I started to think that perhaps Simone de Beauvoir was wrong about not having children, and in any case I never wanted to do exactly what Simone said because Simone said it. I disagreed with her not only about children, but about other things too. I mean, she was not that feminist at the beginning of her life, as I was when I was in my twenties. I thought she could have been a little more feminist and much more concerned with the problem of women in society when she was younger.

I went to study in Chile because I wanted to be more in touch with Latin American women within their own culture, to understand their position in society better and what you could really do for them. If I had gone to Europe I would have become a European, I would have lost touch, particularly when I was so young. To follow Simone because she did certain things for herself; I think it's wrong for everybody to do the same. For another generation, another time in history, it might be different.

I was so pleased when I had my daughter. I had to spend nine months in bed because I have problems about having children, which were only discovered when I could not get pregnant. I felt isolated because I was away from all my family and my Argentinian friends, but I was delighted, particularly because she was a girl. Yanina was born in Concepción, Chile, in 1973.

Shortly after she was born the coup occurred in Chile. After the coup they asked the foreigners who lectured at the university to go to the police. Instead of doing that, I went into hiding with my little girl. My husband was hiding somewhere else in the same city. I was extremely afraid because our house had been ransacked and everything destroyed the night after the coup happened. The armed forces occupied the flat and they tore down nearly everything, including the walls.

I went to spend that night at the house of some of my students, and I saw the news on television. I was absolutely horrified – being an Argentinian, I had some experience of what could happen. I knew this man would be in power for at least twenty years, and it would be cruel. There would be something extremely wrong in Chile, so I went to the police station the next morning because I wanted to register myself, although I gave them a false address. The man who took down my address was the cousin of someone I worked with. I think he was a little sympathetic – he realized I was lying, but he didn't take it any further.

I thought that my daughter and I could be killed. I knew that people had been murdered, the news was passed from mouth to mouth in the streets. You couldn't go out of the house, for instance, without asking permission from someone only ten metres away, and they were using machine guns. When I went to the police station to register my name, I heard them talking amongst themselves about how many people they had killed. The man said to me, 'If you manage to get to your house and collect the baby's clothes before half past twelve you won't be killed, but if you go after that I don't know what will happen to you. My men will have arrived by then . . .'

I was preparing to go into hiding when luckily my father-in-law arrived with seven of his children. As we went down the stairs, an army patrol came through the door. The army patrol said, 'Good morning, sir.'

A few days later I took a special photograph of Yanina so that she could be found if something happened to me or to her. At that time the children were disappearing as well as the adults – children were taken particularly if they didn't find the parents. So Yanina could have been taken in order to see where her father was, if I had disappeared. Things like that happened all the time.

I was arrested and when I left the concentration camp in Chile, they told us that we had forty-eight hours to say our farewells before we were taken to Argentina. But the army officers told us to be very cautious when we went to our house, because another patrol could come, not knowing that I had been **87** through all the procedures, take me into prison again and even kill me or make me 'disappear'. The whole thing could start again. So when I went to my house it was only for twenty minutes or so. I saw my house for the last time, and it's really bad – you feel really bad about it. I had to leave everything behind except some of Yanina's things. Then I chose small things that I thought the army would allow me to take.

I had to leave all Simone de Beauvoir's books behind – at that time I wanted to disassociate myself from them, because they were viewed as subversive by the army. I didn't want to be recognized as the owner of the books!

We lost everything in 1973. It still happens that I go to look for a tablecloth or something and find it's not here – I left it in Chile or somewhere. For a number of years you wake up in the morning and you don't know what country you're in. Sometimes when I go out and people talk in English I am surprised.

I was expelled from Chile with sixteen other adults and eighteen children. We were driven away in an army truck that broke down during a storm in the Andes. I took another photograph of the baby then, to have a last picture of her. I said, 'Well, all of us are going to die, but someone might find these pictures of Yanina.' She was so cold, she was only nine months old, and there was no food for her. Finally the Argentinian army rescued us. All of us survived.

When I was in prison I thought a lot about what Simone said about the Resistance, how she had gone through the period of the war, and this gave me a lot of consolation. I was not allowed to read anything, but I remembered that she had written about women tortured in Algeria, and this gave me much encouragement as well. During those days of repression, when I saw people tortured, raped, and so on, it gave me great comfort to remember that Simone herself had been involved in helping women in that sort of situation.

She has always been for me someone who cares very strongly about other people. People like her are very important for the survival of other individuals. I'm sure that if she had known about what was happening to me she would have helped me, and this is very important in a survival situation. To know that, if you die, someone will know what you have died for. It is so important, and I'm sure she has helped the people of Chile.

After we were expelled from Chile we lived for two and a

half years in Argentina, till there was a coup there too, in 1976. A fortnight later my husband was kidnapped and 'disappeared'. He was a political prisoner for eight months, then expelled officially from Argentina with his family. We asked for exile to Great Britain and several other countries, but the army in Argentina decided to send us to Great Britain. I was given one hour to leave Argentina on 11 November 1976. I went to the airport with Yanina and took the first plane I was directed to. My husband was on it. We came to London first, to say thank-you to all the people who had helped us – from the World University Service, Amnesty International, and church organizations committed to the problems of Argentina and Chile. From there, we went to live in Glasgow, because my husband had been offered a job at Glasgow University. The British Government gave us official refugee status but now I am applying for a reversion of that decision, as I would like to be a British citizen, not a stateless person.

Tomas, my son, was born in Glasgow one year after we arrived, in 1977. We had a lot of support from the local community and also from the people engaged in the Chile Solidarity Campaign and the Scottish Argentina Solidarity Campaign. Everyone in Glasgow is extremely friendly – I didn't speak one word of English at that time, and hardly understood anything in Glaswegian, but they helped me and the little boy to survive. I was pleased to have a boy after having a girl first. My close relationship with Tomas and Yanina has proved to be one of the most rewarding experiences of my life.

The Second Sex meant a lot to me. It was and still is the best book that I have read about women's problems. She summarized brilliantly the way in which different schools of thought view women, and it helped me at the very beginning of my career to realize what my future could be. What she said about professional women has been very important for me since I read the book in 1963 – so that's a long time. It was of tremendous importance for my PhD as well. I wrote a thesis about female social consciousness during the government of Eva and Juan Peron in Argentina, and I used a lot of her ideas about the way women are located and treated in society.

The other thing which gave me a lot to think about in *The Second Sex* was the discussion about women's subordination in **89** so-called socialist societies and whether they would automatically bring about women's liberation. I used everything which was written in that book in my political life. I know there are a lot of problems in it, but I have learned a lot from it.

I'm rebuilding my collection of de Beauvoir books. I've bought *The Second Sex* again, but I'm collecting them very slowly, because to be honest I always think that my books are going to be taken from me. We had three thousand or so books lost in Chile, and then I lost everything again in Argentina – all our records, books, most of our photographs.

Nine years ago I decided to put together my knowledge of what I think about the political problems of Latin American women in a thesis. Quite recently I got my PhD in Development Studies. Eventually I will make it into a book. I would like to dedicate it to Simone because this is the best way for me to keep in touch with her, to do something for her, really. I think it's better than keeping the books together, to make the books come alive.

Eva Figes

8
Eva Figes

Just after the war, when I was an undergraduate, I remember seeing short films in the cinema about Left Bank life, with Juliette Greco in black trousers talking about existentialism, and of course I didn't understand what it was all about, but it looked very trendy and exciting. The books and Cocteau films that came out in the fifties – I found all that very exciting. I suppose as an adolescent I modelled myself on the idea of being avant-garde and daring. I used to wear slinky black trousers and I had long ear-rings and a pony tail.

I can't remember when I read *The Mandarins*; I think by the time I read *The Second Sex* I was already married, but I was certainly aware of de Beauvoir and Sartre as a famous couple, even if I wasn't reading her. I was aware of them as the popular image of intellectuals. Writers in relationships as a couple were very interesting to me. Their relationship was immensely unconventional by the standards of the time. It struck me as a wonderful relationship in the sense that they worked together and yet they had separate apartments and left each other free – at least that was the way it was projected. I thought this was probably the ideal way for a man and woman to live together, by not living together. Later, of course, I discovered that this was all a bit of a sham.

I changed my attitude to their relationship when I realized this; I thought that de Beauvoir was being dishonest, in the sense that she was *not* free, she was living that way because Sartre wanted it. So I changed my views on it. I'm not saying that I don't think it's a good way for a couple to have a relationship over a lifetime – I've never tried it so I don't know – but I did think that she was dishonest about it. I think she was always at Sartre's beck and call, but if she had other relationships in her life, however passionate they may have been, they were while she was 'allowed out', so to speak, and if he said, 'Come back home', she came. We know that did in fact happen with the

Nelson Algren relationship, and I don't call that a free and equal relationship. Whether a free and equal relationship is ever possible, of course, is another question, but she projects the idea that it *is* possible and clearly in her case that was not so. She more or less procured young women for him and that kind of thing. God knows how she felt about it, but she could not have felt equanimity, even if she projects that in her writing.

I married very young by today's standards – I was twenty-one when I met my husband, and we were married when I was twenty-two and he was twenty-three. We were both inexperienced in the ways of the world and of the opposite sex, but in those days it was pretty unusual for anyone to live together without getting married, and I don't think it ever entered our heads not to get married. My first child was born when I was twenty-five.

I worked before and after having my children – I had been working in publishing, so I did freelance work at home. I read unsolicited manuscripts, and solicited ones as well, and I also began to do translations and stuff like that, which I could do at home. I earned a little money, but not enough to live on. When my marriage broke up I was thirty, with two small children, so I then had to go back to work full-time. I went back into publishing, which was the only thing I knew about. It wasn't terribly well-paid, but either publishing or writing has been my life.

I had wanted to write ever since I was a child. I used to write poetry and plays when I was a student, then I had a fallow period when the children were being born, and I didn't know really what direction to take. After my second child was born I began to realize that prose was the thing for me, and I began to think of ways of doing it, but I didn't have anything published until well after my divorce, because that was a sort of beginning phase for me. So my first book was published in 1966 – I had already been a single parent for three years by that time.

While I was writing *Patriarchal Attitudes* I thought I would find *The Second Sex* a useful source book, but then when I began to read it I realized it was totally useless, and I actually stopped reading it. This surprised me, because in fact there were no other books then apart from Betty Friedan, and my first task was to re-read *The Second Sex*. I found for what I wanted to say and the way I wanted to say it, it was of no use to me whatsoever.   **93**

For a start, it seemed to belong to another age. I think one of the problems with de Beauvoir is that she has this tendency to be encyclopaedic, and I wanted to be short and incisive and make political points; I wasn't really interested in gathering loads and loads of information. I also found that she was very ambivalent about female sexuality, and one of the things I wanted to do was to criticise the whole Freudian analysis of women and psychology. On that score she is ambivalent, to say the least. She uses Hélène Deutsch, for example, as though she were pretty well gospel, and I found all this quite disturbing. I put the book aside and I actually found Betty Friedan, with all its limitations, much more useful as a starting point than Simone de Beauvoir.

I feel that de Beauvoir thinks men are superior, and she really does tend to feel that if we could only put aside our physique and all that goes with it, we could be just as good as men. That is not my attitude at all. Also, obviously the whole business of motherhood is something that, having no personal experience of, she has consciously rejected – and that to me was very important. I had already had two children when I wrote *Patriarchal Attitudes*, so unlike a lot of my contemporaries I had no wish to reject that aspect of women's experience. On the contrary, I think one should think about it positively; it's one of the most rewarding experiences in life, even though it takes its toll.

I also felt that her attitude to female sexuality is extremely ambivalent, and I realize with hindsight that as a young woman I had been baffled and bewildered by what she had to say at a time when my knowledge of my own body was limited, to say the least. In the early fifties one of the great questions being asked was, 'Are women frigid, and if so why?' I mean, it really was a huge debating point, and a lot of books were written about it. De Beauvoir does not help to answer that question at all, she tends to say things like, 'Well, a lot of women are quite happy if they just feel nice all over.' There is nothing definite about women's orgasms. That, of course, was one of the big debating points in another sense in the seventies, when people like me were writing about women. I think it was unhelpful, because far from giving one any clear, decisive answers, it just muddied the water still further.

Another aspect where I found her bewildering was the

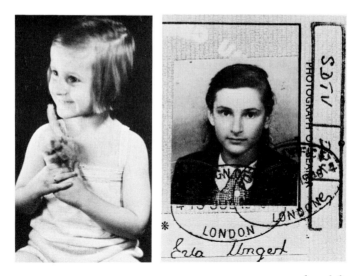

above left
Eva Figes as a child, in Germany

above right
Eva's childhood passport photograph

below
As a teenager

left
In costume for a role in an
amateur drama production

below
With her daughter, Kate

whole question of masochism, in the sense that she writes as though women were actually masochistic, as if it were part of their make-up. I find that unhelpful as well. I think in a way it perpetuates a male myth that women like to get hurt, whether emotionally or physically.

My aims when I wrote *Patriarchal Attitudes* were very different to de Beauvoir's in *The Second Sex*. I wanted specifically to change the system, to change people's attitudes, to get the laws on certain things changed. I used scholarship and scholarly argument simply to drive a point home, I wasn't interested in getting the philosophical thing going, or saying everything that could possibly be said on any one topic. I don't think de Beauvoir's aim was to change laws or to change behaviour and attitudes. She was saying everything that could be said on various aspects of being a woman.

I feel that she not only worshipped Sartre, but worshipped the kind of attitudes and behaviour and cultural standards that men like him project. What she really feels is that women may be at a disadvantage because of their biology, but biology can be overcome up to a point, and we are obviously subject to social conditioning as well . . . She doesn't turn the whole thing on its head, and assert what's so good about being a woman.

Her fiction and autobiography rather merge into each other, because a lot of the fiction is so clearly based on her personal life. On the whole I think her autobiography is more interesting than the fiction because in the fiction she is a rather conventional writer – she doesn't try new forms, she is not lyrical, for instance, she is not a modernist, and therefore one gets more out of the non-fiction.

I do like the book she wrote about her mother's death, and I think one of the reasons I like it is because it is so short. I tend to like things that are brief and incisive, and this one is – it doesn't try to score political points and it isn't as voluminous as some of her work. It's also a very honest book, unsentimental but very moving too.

> And even if death were to win, all this odious deception! Maman thought that we were with her, next to her; but we were already placing ourselves on the far side of her history. An evil all-knowing spirit, I could see behind the scenes, **97**

while she was struggling, far, far, away, in human loneliness. Her desperate eagerness to get well, her patience, her courage – it was all deceived. She would not be paid for any of her sufferings at all. I saw her face again: 'Since it is good for me.' Despairingly, I suffered a transgression that was mine without my being responsible for it and one that I could never expiate.

from *A Very Easy Death*

I used to see her as a sort of role model as a writer in society; I felt very strongly when I began to publish books that I didn't want only to write novels. I felt that in order to be a real writer I had to be politically involved (I now think that this is not the only alternative). I wanted to write political stuff, to be 'engaged' in the French sense. One of the reasons I left my job in the sixties was that I felt I didn't just want to publish a novel every two years, I wanted to do other things as well. I was ready for it, and to do that I would need to be a writer full-time. When I did that, I was really thinking of de Beauvoir – I thought that was the kind of person I wanted to be, a writer who is involved in every sense, not only politically but as a human being as well.

I think for women it is easier to be a writer, or any kind of career woman, if you don't have a live-in husband or lover as well, because unfortunately the way things still are, men can't tolerate this very easily; they do expect a wife or girlfriend to revolve around them a little bit and cater to their needs. This makes life quite hard for a professional woman and I think particularly hard for a writer, because you need inner space as well as outer space – you need time to think your own thoughts and meditate, in a sense. I often think it's not so much the time you spend at the typewriter but the time you spend staring out of the window that is really the most productive, and the ability to close yourself off from human contact for a while is very important in the creative process. That is easier to achieve if you are on your own. When you have young children, you still have the problem, of course, of finding time and space and a little bit of quiet, but that is easier to arrange. You can always tell your children to be quiet and go to bed, but you can't really tell that to an adult male – not easily, anyway.

Oscar Wilde said, 'The only thing to do with good advice is

to pass it on.' As far as my daughter is concerned, I think it's important for a woman to have some kind of career structure, whether you are married and have children or not. Children are only lent to us anyway, they grow up and you shouldn't invest everything in your children. It's very important for a woman to have some kind of career that engrosses her. I also think you need a safety net financially because nobody can say whether the marriage will last for ever, for whatever reason – there is death as well as divorce, all sorts of things can happen. I think a woman should not make herself totally dependent on a man, even less make herself and her family dependent on a man, because that can lead to a lot of problems.

Certainly in some areas of work the marketplace for jobs is now much more flexible and much more open to women than when I was young, and the idea of women working is now totally taken for granted. The only way I could get a job at one stage, when I was a single parent, was by assuring them that as I was divorced and I already had two children, I wasn't likely to go off and get married and have another baby, so therefore I might actually stay in the job. That kind of attitude I hope is no longer so prevalent as it was.

I think my daughter reckons feminism has moved on since I wrote *Patriarchal Attitudes*. She regards me as what she calls the 'first wave'. I think the first wave was an important wave. I tend to feel that feminism has lost its way rather at the moment, partly because of the overall political situation. I mean, you have to remember that feminism started as an end result of the sixties, which were a liberation in many ways and people were very hopeful then about the future. Now we are into a very right-wing, reactionary stage and that makes feminism direc-tionless in the sense that the kind of demands we were making twenty years ago are no longer feasible. I think if feminism is to get anywhere, it should be concentrating on things like equal opportunities, equal pay, crèches for children and those kinds of social things that can actually make life easier for women and their families, and other things should be left to the personal sphere and not really the political.

I have no doubt that de Beauvoir, both as a writer and certainly in terms of political influence, will be seen as more significant than Sartre at the end of the day. I believe feminism is one of the **99** few radical movements that is here to stay, unlike a lot of left-wing movements, which died the death for various historical reasons. Her influence on the feminist movement is bound to have a much greater effect than any of the things that Sartre did politically, and also I think that probably apart from a few of his plays, her writing is more interesting too. Certainly the other stuff he wrote would be consigned to a few footnotes, and a few students might wallow through all those volumes on Flaubert, but I doubt if anyone else would be very interested. It's one of the ironies that she should have worshipped her male partner so much when in fact she is clearly by far the more important person in the long run.

Joyce Goodfellow

9
Joyce Goodfellow

As a young woman (you were young longer then than you are today) I did rather resent the questions neighbours used to ask my parents, like, 'Isn't your daughter getting married yet, hasn't she got a boyfriend?' and that sort of thing. I thought, 'I don't want all those things, there must be something wrong with me.' I left school quite early, principally to earn some money – a pittance but it felt like freedom. About the time *The Second Sex* was published, when I was about twenty, I read anything I could find. The cover attracted me, with that nude lady, and I thought 'I will see what this is about,' and of course I really jumped in at the deep end. She seemed to give me some sort of permission to be the kind of person I wanted to be; I thought, 'Someone else has felt this way.'

Due to the fact that I was a working class girl and had been educated during the war, I didn't have a lot of contact with philosophy, so I read it in isolation. I showed it to a few friends, who weren't very interested. It was a shock that this French woman had this view of the female not as a 'Mummy person' but as someone who could be free. I accepted this idea but I didn't have the resources to cope with it. I thought, 'I don't have to get married, I can move into this world where the French films are, with dinner parties and wine and the obligatory black person and lots of interesting conversation.' But I hadn't realized, and didn't realize it for years, that the woman who had written the book was a very educated woman from a comfortable background. She was living with a very famous intelligent person who was helping her and I really hadn't got a hope in hell of moving into this world. Unaware of this, I took the idea on board, looking for this sort of life where you could talk about yourself as a person and admit that all sorts of things happen to your emotions, to your body, and you didn't have to gloss over them. You could say words like 'pregnant'. I mean, in our street they didn't say that, they used to say, 'She's . . . you know,' like Les Dawson does now.

So I went from there, with this idea having been put into my consciousness, and made a terrible mess of things. I went from job to job, tried travel agencies as I had a desire to travel, and ended up doing the filing. I just was not educated.

I very much fancied going on the stage and managed to get into a repertory company as an unpaid assistant – it was dogsbody sort of thing. I didn't see that if I wanted journalism, fame, travel, excitement, you actually had to get trained up for it, or get adopted by a wonderful person who would do it for you, as lots of people have been by men who found them and said, 'This is an interesting lady.' Well, that didn't happen to me.

In pursuit of my idea of travel I moved from the travel agency into the WRNS. I now loathe all things military, but at the time I thought I should travel. I didn't. I was a writer, they called it a writer, in an office in Chatham, which is a very boring place. However I did meet a person doing his National Service to whom I became engaged. Then I discovered that he didn't have the right ideas. We saw a film with Anna Magnani called *The Small Miracle* where an Italian peasant woman gave birth to a child in a cave on a hill, and it could have been another Christ. I was deeply moved by the notion that this was possible, but he said, 'What a load of rubbish, it was that shepherd who made her pregnant.' I thought, 'I can't marry this man, he doesn't have my kind of ideas.' I think he didn't realize that in being engaged to me he had a problem, that I wasn't looking to be a housewife in Manchester or anything like that, so I broke it off and he never really understood why.

After I left the WRNS and broke off my engagement, I met a person who was very influential in my life, a man with a great intellect – he was in fact an artist. We were very happy and we were very unhappy. After a while it turned out that he was married and his religion forbade any further marriage – he had not lived with his own family for some years. There was no question of a divorce, and at that time I was in the sort of world in which I wanted to be, the people I met were very interesting, I could feel my ideas expanding, and I had a good time. It was wonderful, but it couldn't last.

The thing I hadn't caught on to with de Beauvoir was that it was essential not to have any children. Now, working it out in retrospect, I can see many facets to this decision on her part. I hadn't made this decision, however. I did have a baby, and I found that it is very difficult to be an emancipated woman if you have the responsibility for another life. I mean, I quite fancied being a Colin Wilson 'outsider', but careful scrutiny of this will reveal that most of them are men – so what I was finding out was that you can't be an outsider if you breed. I was finding all this out by experience, not by reading about it. I had to try everything.

For some years I had a relationship with this man. In order to fit in with our lifestyle I became an artist's model. I had independence, it's very hard work, and it was in fact very interesting. I modelled when pregnant, I modelled with the new baby, and I think the art school students were all very grateful for this opportunity. But it was about half a crown an hour, so I had to go back into the world of the office in order to support the child. I lived with my mother, I had to support the child, I had to pay my mother, and I went back to an office job. I still talked about books I had read, ideas that I had and so on, and was thought a bit peculiar. I did wretched jobs like the filing, the tea, errands, and so on.

But here I met the man whom I married. He seemed strangely interested in the artist, the baby's father, and we all used to go out with another girl. My husband-to-be found this all very interesting, I think it was a world he had been attracted to and I was a way into it. Ultimately he asked me to marry him. I was still very doubtful about being married and broke off the engagement, but he insisted it would be all right, so we were married. But it wasn't all right.

I still doubted that I was cut out for domesticity, but I took that chance. He enjoyed the interesting life, but of course, having stepped across into the world of mortgages and do-it-yourself, the interesting life started to fade out again, which may have disappointed him and certainly disappointed me. We then had a son, and he wasn't very thrilled about that, either.

My daughter has said to me, 'Why didn't you first of all discuss how many children you wanted?' I told her that you didn't lead your life in that way in those days, you didn't say to each other what you would do. It was all a bit haphazard. Anyway, I thought, this is wonderful, we are four, we are a

family, I have got what I didn't think I wanted, but perhaps I

top
Joyce Goodfellow as a young
girl with her parents

above
During World War II

right
In the WRNS

above left
With her baby son

above right
At a fun-fair with her lover.

below
With her lover and their daughter

shall like it. But it all started to go terribly wrong. He didn't like having all these kids around.

Eventually my husband left me. He had complained (it was very funny, he was always good at black humour), 'They say that intellectuals have dirty taps. What's your excuse?' He meant that I had failed in both fields. I was no intellectual, no one paid me for all these poems that I wrote and these evening classes and all these strange ideas, and I didn't clean the home either. He did meet another lady who I think was very efficient. He left his office, he was doing very well and making a lot of money, and he decided to train as a teacher. My lover had been an art teacher.

The Second Sex became embedded in my consciousness. I didn't read the autobiographies (I'm saving them for my retirement) because Simone de Beauvoir has done quite enough harm already. I read some of her novels, but I didn't feel they had anything to do with her – this emancipated lady. They were all about sex and jealousy. I thought these were just clever novels and everyone was in a terrible state. They weren't supposed to feel like this – they were supposed to accept all these things like having an open marriage, and no one was to be jealous. But you couldn't; I knew what it was like to be jealous. There is cool logic and warm life, two totally different things.

What a difference it would have made if de Beauvoir and Sartre had had children, (was she sterilized at twenty or something, what did the woman *do*?). You can't imagine it, really. Either they would have been amazing people, the children of this astonishing couple, or they would have destroyed the home and the relationship entirely. I think it's called *égoïsme à deux* when you just have the two of you with no interferences, and I think she seemed so destroyed by jealousy, which she only brings into her novels, and, later, by the death of her mother, that she couldn't cope with the real emotional blows (no more than I can). Due to her giving me a little push, I have had to cope with the blows, but she stayed there (on the ice cold peaks?) supported and with money. I never had any money. People put out these ideas and they don't carry health warnings. I know it was my own problem and not really the problem of Simone, but these ideas are a problem without some intelligent mentor **107** saying, 'Well, you must have a good education, you must work very hard.'

If I was really going to follow her advice in the book, it would have been best not to have had children. These were the things that I should have done, but I didn't know it. I think it was reading the book in isolation, rather than reading it as a set text at university with other people around to discuss it with that caused me to be so deeply influenced.

I think that I would say my life has been interesting, perhaps with a capital 'I', but I don't think it's been fair on the children. Essentially I have got what I wanted; as the proverb has it, 'Be very careful what you want because you will probably get it.' The children grew up and left home – well, one is hanging on tenaciously, but that's because he's lazy. I didn't marry again, I thought clearly that was not for me, not for anyone that might be involved with me. So now I am sixty, and I am alone. And this gives me a great deal of freedom to do many things, except I don't have any money and I have rather a horrible home. Obviously, you get what you want – I don't mind too much about the horrible home – but people who are still married, frequently not happily, say, 'I would never break it up, this is my home and this is where I stay. If I can't bear the arguing any more we go into different rooms.' This is true, persons of my age who are married, some are happy and some are not, but they don't give up their home. I have done this, and I am partly happy and partly unhappy.

They say to me, 'I wish I had your freedom.' I say to them, 'Why aren't you trying it?' But they say they don't want to. I am now at such a vast distance from my first reading of *The Second Sex* that I am able to see very clearly how it encouraged me to be a different sort of person, prematurely. If it encourages other women today, I think they would be a bit more on the ball to really work out how you would lead that kind of life. I didn't do this, so I'm a bit angry with the de Beauvoir philosophy, which she pursued childless, with the help of a man. She had a good home, a good education, she was not poor. Yet you do embrace both poverty and solitude because you are making it yourself, not as the other half of a couple.

It becomes increasingly difficult to find people with the right attitude because men are not struggling to be free, they *are* free. Had I been a man, I might have succeeded in my enterprises. I had a male cousin who joined a ship at fourteen, travelled the world and ended up as a captain. He did everything he wanted to do, and retired peacefully to his home and family. But I feel I never made it, I kept climbing up a glass mountain, and the climbing was nice and the sliding back was nasty, and now I am in this curious isolated landscape where I still read a lot and I am still joining pottery classes and doing new things. Some of my attitudes have passed on to my children – they travel, my daughter is in the media, in drama and entertainment, and she nurtures some of the ideas which I had, but she's not much impressed with de Beauvoir. She's got the outline of it all from me, but she says, 'That's stupid, you couldn't do that. You should have educated yourself.' They do see more clearly. They decide about children, they *can* decide, there is the pill and they defer them until they are thirty. I think they are further down the road in the right direction. But they're still going to have problems, and de Beauvoir is no longer with us and can't answer the accusations.

I feel the book should carry a health warning: 'Beware of breeding: it cramps ambition, intellectual opportunity and the bank balance, and it isn't fair to the children. Remember that life is very long and while you're pursuing diverse paths and laughing at mortgages and dry rot, you may end up in an old folks' home, and you may become isolated.' I don't know. I am still confused. I feel that de Beauvoir was helping me to be confused because I couldn't cope with her material, and so I assimilated it and probably made mistakes, but I couldn't see how many worlds away from me this woman was. It was translated into my language, it was on my bookstall for 2/6d or whatever, and it didn't carry a warning, 'This is not for you'. I can't blame her. But I think that partly it made me the odd person that I am. What you read really does influence your life.

It has all been very interesting. I don't think I can say that *The Second Sex* has done me any positive good. I can only use the word 'interesting'. Interesting book, interesting life, but perhaps not really advisable. Simone always had someone to support her. I haven't had, nor have lots of people, and I think that is why I get angry. She didn't say, 'Most people need someone to lean on from time to time.' I just found myself falling over, and, more like a Thomas Hardy heroine than a de Beauvoir one, I **109** rejected all support systems and fell, it seemed deliberately, into disaster. Beware of blue stockings if you can't afford them; they can make you seem a freak, or maverick.

Marge Piercy

10
Marge Piercy

I considered myself an existentialist in my senior year at college. It was around 1956, and I believe I read Sartre first, in French class – we read a play of his, and I was taken by it, and then I read whatever I could lay my hands on. The first thing of Simone de Beauvoir's I read was *The Ethics of Ambiguity*, which I liked enormously. Because we couldn't study existentialism formally then, in my senior year we started an informal seminar with a graduate student. I was in English Honours, and a lot of my friends were Philosophy Honours.

I had seen photographs of Juliette Greco, and that get-up was perfect for me, because I was very poor. I was the first of my family to go to college. The way college girls dressed then was in pleated skirts and cashmere sweater sets and pearls, or very dressy little suits. Well, I had none of that gear. However, I could perfectly well dress as an existentialist in nothing at all – in black jeans, a black turtleneck, my hair down and a lot of dark red lipstick and eye make-up, so it was perfect for me. Not only was it aesthetically satisfying, but it was dirt cheap – and it didn't show the dirt, for that matter. It was just perfect.

She Came to Stay was the first of the novels I read and I was enormously struck by the fluidity and the realism in the relationships. I got very excited about her and from that time on I remained primarily interested in her. In graduate school at Northwestern I studied existentialism more formally, and Heidegger and Kierkegaard and Sartre and so forth, but she meant an awful lot to me, from that time on. When her memoirs began to appear I read them, and I read the novels as they came out, and then I read *The Second Sex*.

What was so forceful to me about her, first of all, was that she was of the Left. The Left in the United States at that time was non-existent, except for a sort of persecuted Communist minority, and Stalinism wasn't very interesting. Most of the old Left were fighting among themselves, and seemed rather quaint and unrelated to what we were trying to do. It all seemed to have very little to do with the sense of injustice I had, or the kind of union battles we'd grown up with in Detroit, or the anti-Semitism I experienced very freely, growing up in Detroit, or my situation as a woman, which nothing spoke to, until I read her.

She was dealing with the effort to behave justly and politically, and not to forget about people. One of the things that struck me about *The Ethics of Ambiguity*, and which I think was important in the long run for me, was that she kept saying you don't erect values as absolutes, or ideals as absolutes; you always remember that whatever you're doing, you're doing it for people. If you're sacrificing something, you're sacrificing people for that something; to will yourself free is to will other people free. That became one of the mottoes I lived by, and still live by, that you respect other people as real beings, whatever political decisions you're making.

Unlike most of the women I was in college with, who came from middle-class backgrounds, I came from a working-class background. I'd been sexually active much earlier than they had. I'd had a lot more experiences. Everything in the culture told me I was going to die of this rather speedily. The Freudian set and the conservative set then just said that a woman couldn't do anything except marry, presumably a middle-class husband, live in a nice house in the suburbs and have three children as rapidly as possible, or you go crazy, you would die horribly, or you'd dry up into something strange and desiccated.

By my senior year I was probably rather nervous about the fact that I'd had all these adventures that I wasn't supposed to have had. When I got married, I married many things. I married France, the Left, Jews who had survived the war . . . I also married a particular French physicist, and that was the problem! It turned out to be a very conventional, bourgeois marriage.

For a while I thought, 'Well this might work out for me, maybe there'll be enough psychological space.' But by the end of the second year of the marriage it was very clear that there was no space for me. Whatever I wanted to do, you didn't do it like that. Whatever I wanted to be, you couldn't be like that. That summer I was coming to the conclusion that this was not a road I was prepared to go down any further. I read *The Second Sex* and   113 there on the flyleaf it says, 'Chicago, 1959.' And I can find in my early copies of her books all these funny little marginal annotations of my life at that time. I can trace things I've forgotten about. Sometimes what I wrote in the margins about relationships and about people was very self-judgemental. I was always trying to decide if I was ethical or not, or aggressive enough in pursuing my values, or giving enough to my writing.

The fact was, I had moved from a high-visibility position in Michigan as a student who won a lot of awards and was the author of pieces in literary magazines, to being a wife, where I suddenly became invisible, and when I went into the workforce as a secretary, I became totally invisible. When you opened your mouth and said things, nobody could hear you any more. That was rather interesting to me – the loss of position, and a sense of culture in your life, shortly after marrying.

I was thinking about all these things, but it was a formless kind of musing. I had no way to think analytically. Nobody said it was because I was a woman. I kept thinking, what's happened? I open my mouth and speak and nobody hears me any more. I move in a room, and I'm invisible; what has happened? In *The Second Sex* de Beauvoir provided an analysis for experiences that were familiar to me, but if you do not have a vocabulary, you cannot handle your own experience. One of the things that feminism does for women is that it names things. Once you name something, it exists for you, you can handle it in your mind, you can turn it around, you can decide what to do about it. But if things have no names, all you can do is feel a sense of uneasiness. It's a personal thing then: instead of being an issue, it's your own problem – 'Why do *I* feel weird? Why do I feel strange? What did *I* do?' So it was very important to me in marshalling my resources to move forward in a direction that appeared to everyone around me as jumping off a cliff. But to me it meant freedom, it meant the autonomy to do my own work.

She also provided a kind of role model, for years, because she wrote both politically and as a woman, and there was very little political fiction going on in the United States. Everything in English departments was designed to deal with the experiences of an English gentleman. But I would never be an English gentleman. I was not Anglo-Catholic like Eliot, and I wasn't going to carry a black umbrella the way I saw all the guys doing in graduate school. Where was I to look? Well, there she was.

Marge Piercy as a student in her 'existentialist' days

She was both writing politically and writing about being a woman, writing seriously about the relationships between women, and love relationships, friendship relationships, mother-daughter relationships both on a personal level and on a larger level. She was able to take the larger view and the long view, and yet not lose the sense of the reality of relationships, the warmth of daily life. I didn't see anyone else doing things like that.

This combination was stunning to me and exciting. It represented a door. And her life, too, as the memoirs began to come out, represented a way of life in which a woman had chosen to be in relationships, multiple relationships, and yet remain committed to her own work, committed to her own politics, to retain her sense of integrity without giving up life as a woman, and to remain open throughout her life to new experiences, new people, to constant growth and political change. All of that was tremendously exciting and moving to me. It was a great example.

For all that, I never mistake myself for somebody else; I mean everybody makes their own choices. She had a central relationship which after a short time was not a sexual relationship, but which defined her life – her thoughts, her projects were all shared with Sartre. I never wanted anybody at the centre of my life like that. I never wanted to share my work. My work is at the centre of my life and the intellectual space around that is very jealously guarded.

My second marriage was not a marriage as most people use the term. It was an open relationship, and at any given year in it we might be separated, we might be living with other people, there might be other people with us. The most important relationships were not necessarily with each other, and indeed in the best part of that connection we didn't even see a tremendous amount of each other. We would have to make appointments to see each other, actually.

I lived for about fifteen years of my adult life in multiple relationships, that is, not with one central relationship. Others were peripheral or casual, but I lived in what I used to call a matrix of relationships: there were a number of very serious, important, valued and loving relationships. In a sense, that belonged to the time, it belonged to the era of the 1960s and 1970s. You sort of can't do it now, but that was the way I lived for many years. It was decentralized and communal, far more than her life was.

So with any life – it's all organized in a particular way. In her memoirs she organizes her life around her relationship with Sartre. Another woman, with different values, would have viewed that relationship as more peripheral, because when it ceased to be a sexual relationship it would have become less central. Indeed her life could have been organized more in terms of serial-monogamy, in which the relationship with Nelson Algren, for instance, would then have been tremendously important.

I'm very interested in the relationship with Lanzmann, because he seemed to me a warmer person than Sartre. I was always interested in the way in which she structured the myth of the relationship with Sartre. Not that I'm saying it wasn't a tremendously important relationship to her, but as a novelist I'm always aware, as I'm sure she was, of the way she reworked the same material, in the novels and in the memoirs, in very different ways. Looking at anything in life, you can structure it. Just like after a coup, history is rewritten because it comes out differently. Similarly, very frequently people re-write their lives after a relationship has ended. You build in the causes for that ending. It then becomes a fatal tragedy leading towards a dissolution, then comes the victory of the next relationship, and so on, but she didn't organize her life that way. She met Sartre early, she put him at the centre of her life, and he remained at the centre of her life – at the same time as she lived with Lanzmann, not with Sartre, for eight years.

You can never tell in autobiography when someone is being candid or when they are simply playing with certain themes from their life. Writing fiction has its own requirements. When you fictionalize yourself into a character, as in *L'Invitée*, where the character we assume represents Simone de Beauvoir kills a young woman, we're not to assume that Simone de Beauvoir is concealing evidence of a murder, or even that she truly wished to kill, but that she was interested in exploring some kind of symbolic truth. What would that be like, what does that mean, what would that feel like? Indeed, once you engage in that as a character, the character has its own logic. For myself, my fiction is the lives I haven't lived far more than the lives I have lived. It's others' experiences I'm interested in exploring. I'm sure there's   **117** an element of that in *The Mandarins*, where the central character has children, whereas de Beauvoir didn't.

The fact that she chose not to have children was another reason I identified with her. She was very clear about the choice, very clear about the reasons she was making it, very unapologetic about it. It seemed to me a clear and sunny, rational yet felt choice.

I myself chose not to have children partly from a sense of not wanting to give hostages, so that I would be free to make my own choice and take my own consequences. If you're a political person, that can be very important to you. For instance, once when I was with Margaret Randall in 1968 I saw how her children were vulnerable, and made her vulnerable. That it was dangerous to be her child at that time in Mexico in 1968. It was terrifying. But I also chose not to have children because work is central to me. The work is central, the work is what I do, and that comes before anything else, and it's what gives me supreme satisfaction. I think the work is my children.

Before feminism began again, which I think of as being in 1966, there really was very little that touched on women's lives, that built a fire under you, that enabled you to find a relevant analytical vocabulary. So de Beauvoir had tremendous importance, and her work was so much more global than anyone else's. It was much more ambitious, it was so much more intellectually challenging. That combination of intelligence and not losing the daily reality based in women's experience moved me. Being able to look at institutions through time in a quasi-Marxist way, and then turning and looking at the relationship between sisters, or between mothers and daughters, with the same seriousness, and the same intellectual capacity, the very fresh clear-eyed way she had of looking at things. That I love.

She and Sartre were among the forces that said you're not crazy to be interested in justice; you're not out of your mind, you are not weird, this doesn't make you a Stalinist nut.

I don't think she wrote with working-class women in mind, but that doesn't make her books irrelevant to working-class women, because so many of the situations that she deals with are women's situations. They're different in different classes, but you can use them, you can use her analysis and her ideas.

118   I wouldn't have liked a relationship like she had with Sartre

– no way! Again, the life not lived always fascinates me, and the idea of the total intellectual communication and creative companionship is a fantasy for many women. It's the fantasy of actually being able to talk to a man. You know, you may have communication but it's the idea of the total sharing of the initiatives of creativity. Your life, your politics or your work being open to criticism at that basic level has never appealed to me. I want autonomy; I like silence as well as communication. I like an inner space, which is where my own creativity ferments. I love communication and I love companionship, I'm a very warm person in my relationships with other people, but there's an inner silence, too, which she didn't need in that way. In a way it makes me feel more neutered, more defended than her, but also more solitary in the inner workings of my creativity.

There's a passage in *The Prime of Life* where she sketches that basic myth of the relationship with Sartre, and what she most valued in it:

> To achieve basic understanding with someone is a very rare privilege in any circumstances; for me, it took on a literally infinite value. At the back of my memory there glowed, with unparalleled sweetness, all those long hours that Zaza and I had spent hidden in Monsieur Mabille's study, talking. I too had experienced moments of poignant pleasure when my father smiled at me, and I could tell myself that, in a sense, this peerless man was *mine*. My adolescent dreams projected these supreme moments of my childhood into the future: they were not mere insubstantial fancies, but had a real existence for me – which is why their fulfilment never struck me as miraculous. Certainly circumstances were all in my favour: I might never have found anyone with whom I could reach a state of perfect agreement. When my chance was offered me, I took it; the passion and tenacity with which I did so showed me how deeply rooted the urge was in me.
>
> Sartre was only three years older than I was – an equal, as Zaza had been – and together we set forth to explore the world. My trust in him was so complete that he supplied me with the sort of absolute unfailing security that I had once had from my parents, or from God. When I threw myself into a world of freedom, I found an unbroken

119

sky above my head. I was free of all shackling restraint, and yet every moment of my existence possessed its own inevitability. All my most remote and deep-felt longings were now fulfilled; there was nothing left for me to wish – except that this state of triumphant bliss might continue unwaveringly forever.

from *The Prime of Life*

I'm married to a writer now, Ira Wood, and I have a more intense, more communicative relationship with him than I've ever had with a man. But still the basic political decisions, basic creative decisions, are mine.

Sometimes she even refers to Sartre as being superior to her, and that amazes me. I can't imagine that. That seems to me, in a way, a desire left over from her childhood, as in *Memoirs of a Dutiful Daughter*, where she talks about her father as the one who opens the world, the one who is the more intellectual. I didn't come from that kind of background. My mother never finished the tenth grade, but she was more political, more imaginative, she was more interested in ideas, she read more than my father. I didn't grow up looking to men for ideas. I think as a working-class woman what I expect from a man is quite different often from what middle-class women expect from men. I don't expect guidance, support, being led along. I'm not looking for a father. Maybe I look for a brother, I look for someone to offer warmth, companionship, domestic things.

In fact I think she helped Sartre far more than he helped her. I always thought that, just as Sartreans assume that, you know, she just did a little piece of it or something, I've always thought her intelligence was in his service more than I would have liked it to have been. Though as I say, I have tremendous respect for Sartre also; I came to him first of all and I retain a respect for him. I'm not sure it was the best thing that ever happened to her, but she was convinced of it, and she has to be the expert on her own life.

He certainly wasn't my cup of tea. He was somebody who didn't like his body. When she interviews him in *Adieux*, she's really quite critical, and she pushes him about his relationships with women, what he liked and what he didn't like. He couldn't have been too much fun in bed, I have to say, and I'm sure he didn't have friendships with women. If you weren't involved with him, really you would have had very little to do with him if you were a woman. He had friendships with men, but his friendships with women, as she analyses them in *Adieux*, were always, certainly at first, sexual.

Adieux is very sad. It's a terrifying thing to watch the death of someone that she cared a great deal about, it's impossible not to identify with that, to be frightened, and also to watch the dissolution of the mind, a very creative mind. And a loss of control over the politics, over the creativity, over the thought, and the body, of course. It's a very moving book. And the interviewing between them is extraordinary.

It's different from the autobiographies; it's more critical, maybe because he was dead. In some ways it's less softened, there's less of a scrim through which you're seeing it. The physical facts of the relationship – maybe because it's about death, rather than sex – are right up front. It's a magnificent book. So was the book about her mother's death. It has a similar sort of bodily facticity that the other books don't have. I started to re-read it right after my mother's death but I couldn't. I couldn't. It was too close then. Perhaps I should look at it now.

I met Nelson Algren once. A couple of friends of mine had met him at a literary conference and they set up an evening together. I was this young writer who took herself very seriously, and I was meeting with another writer, and I wanted to talk to him about Simone de Beauvoir. I didn't realize it was a date! He took me to the fights, and to hear jazz, and so forth. It was hysterical. As soon as I started trying to talk about Simone de Beauvoir – it was the last thing in the universe he wanted to talk about, and the last thing he wanted to do was deal with me as a young writer. I was a girl. It was total nonsense. It was one of those situations in which people's expectations are so bizarrely different.

At the same time, I enjoyed talking to him; in some ways we had a certain amount in common. I liked going to the fights, I'd grown up in a neighbourhood where Joe Louis was a big hero, as he was in all the black neighbourhoods in Detroit. Algren lived in the streets, and I came off the streets too; I'd been in a gang, and the world he wrote about wasn't alien to me in any sense.

I never tried to meet Simone de Beauvoir. I always felt that she meant a great deal to me, but that was my business, not hers. **121**

If someone's public work is writing memoirs, their memoirs once created, are an artefact separate from them. They are a piece of art. That's even true of philosophical work and novels, they're separate from you. Other people take the artefact, it belongs to them. All of Simone de Beauvoir that belonged to me, I had: it was the public work which she made out of herself. The fact that someone means a great deal to you doesn't mean you can impinge upon their privacy and say, 'Hey! Here I am, I'm your inheritor, I'm your daughter! You haven't seen me before but listen, I love you, and you'd better love me because you mean a lot to me, and I'm about to make demands on you!' That's horrible.

I did write to her, though, I believe it was after *Vida* came out in French. I just said, 'I want you to have this, you've meant a great deal to me, don't answer this letter.'

I'm not French so I don't know a lot about her relationship with the French women's movement, but a friend who had been over there came back and told me she was letting her apartment be used for illegal abortions, and that she was very involved with the French women's movement. That moved me. I'd been very involved with getting some women abortions when it was illegal, and with the attempt to change the laws, so it was a source of identification and I was moved by her doing that.

The one thing that was exciting about both Sartre and de Beauvoir was that they were constantly able to relate to younger people, to movements; they could even permit themselves to be used. Sartre was used by the Maoists. They were willing to do that and not think it was such a terrible thing. And they recognized that there are different agendas. You can be involved in the same attempt to move history with different means. You don't have to agree with people completely, just give them a little help. That always seemed to me great, that they could remain alive and connected in that way, and that it didn't threaten them that there were people younger than them, which is not always the case with prominent people.

When I heard that she had died, I felt a tremendous sense of loss. A lot of the sense of loss was that there would be no more work, no more volumes of the autobiography; a conversation that had gone on in my head from the time I was twenty years old was silenced. There were no more treasures that would come to me, no more instalments. And, you know, you always fantasize there will be some way to work on something together, there'll be some natural way of coming together without imposing. But basically it was that there would be no more work, and the work always remained so alive, so interesting, so exciting.

Sylvie le Bon de Beauvoir

11
Sylvie le Bon de Beauvoir

I came to Paris to study when I was seventeen, and started writing to Simone de Beauvoir while I was at the Lycée. She replied, and I started seeing her regularly, and after a time we became very close friends, after about five years.

Although I am her adopted daughter, our relationship was quite different from a mother-daughter relationship. This was important to both of us, she was displeased when she heard people call it so, and I was too, because we didn't have that kind of relation at all. We were equals, friends. Because of the difference in our ages, people used to think she was a mother and I was a daughter – but not at all. I admired her very much, but we were friends. We were friends in spite of the difference in age. I never thought of her age, you know, never. But she often thought about it, she used to say, 'I will die before you.'

She liked young people, she knew several students like me, women students, and I think she was looking for the same kind of total friendship she had when she was younger, with her friend Zaza. I think she had a kind of nostalgia for a close, intimate relation with a woman. She had women-friends but they weren't able to discuss things with her. She had Olga, whom she liked very much, but Olga was not an intellectual.

Apart from Sartre, she had Bost, Algren, Lanzmann and so on, very dear friends, but they were all men. She was ten when she discovered she loved Zaza and until Zaza died (at twenty) she was her *alter ego*, and with her she lost something precious. I think she wanted to find this kind of relation again with a woman. She tried several times but it failed for one reason or another, because she wanted a friendship from both the head and the heart. She said, 'I am an intellectual woman, for me they go together, and I want a friend who is also an intellectual.' I think that might explain, from her part, our relationship.

She never wanted children, for several reasons which she explains quite clearly in her books. She wasn't looking for a **125** daughter in me, absolutely not. For me, I was certainly not looking for a mother, because my personal experience with my own mother was very bad, so I didn't want to repeat it. There was an equality between us, although of course I admired her very much as well. I should like to say that she was for me what Sartre was for her: equality, with admiration. Certainly not motherhood. It's easier for the public to see the other through stereotypes. It's terrible because it's quite false, and I'm glad to say here that it was not at all like that. Instead of *given* relations she preferred, like me, *chosen* relations.

I read her novels first, and I was fascinated by her perception of the way other people speak and act. I was also always impressed by the fact that the way she thought and the way she lived were the same, were mixed. I admired her strictness. She always said relations between human beings were not fixed by nature. A man and a woman have to create a relation between them – or a man with another man, why not, and a woman with another woman. Everything is possible. I thought how true this was. I still think it's true now – everything is possible between two or several people, I mean. I found these ideas fascinating, it was more than just ideas, it was a way of life, and when I got to know her it was so easy to pass from the books to the woman: she was familiar at once.

When I read *Memoirs of a Dutiful Daughter* and *The Prime of Life* – the others were not yet written – I liked them very much, I read *The Second Sex* and liked it as a philosophical book, not as a feminist work. It sounds silly; of course, I understood it was feminist, but as I was already a feminist, I should say a 'spontaneous feminist', I was above all interested by the philosophical aspect of the book, the reflective thought – more than by the militant consequences (or involvements). I thought it was luminous but sometimes I was shocked by it, because I was very young and puritan when I read it. I thought it was shocking; she laughed when I told her my reaction. I thought the autobiography was above all very well written, because for me first of all she was a writer, not a feminist. I think she also considered herself first as a writer, and she used to become a little irritated when people saw her only as a feminist.

She wrote about me in her autobiography, in *Tout Compte Fait (All Said and Done)*, which is something of a strange experience. She didn't say much, it wasn't a psycho-analysis or

top
Sylvie le Bon as a child,
and as a student

left
Sylvie on one of her trips
abroad with Simone
de Beauvoir

above
Sylvie with Simone in Paris

anything, but she asked me if I agreed, and she showed me what she had written and we talked about it and made a few changes, but I didn't think there was anything odd about it. That was the risk when you were a writer's friend . . .

We used to travel together a great deal, it was a great pleasure in life for her. We went to many countries, and when we came back from travelling we used to meet Sartre in Rome every year at the end of the holidays. Sartre worked so hard, he didn't go away much, so she went with me because she loved travelling. It was very important for her, a great pleasure, and she travelled very seriously, she wanted to see everything, she never got tired. I used to get tired sometimes, but she never did! The last time we drove a long way was in 1985, to Austria and Hungary, in the summer.

She really loved life, she was always cheerful. She wrote about her life like that, and it was really true, it was apparent to everyone. She liked going to good restaurants, she loved food and good wine and so on. As she wrote, she was gifted for happiness.

She did everything herself, she never had a secretary. She answered almost every letter she received from her readers, she was very well organized. She also knew how to say 'no'; Sartre never did, and he used to get eaten up by people. She worked every day and writing was her life. She was a very hard worker, all her life, as Sartre was too.

When Sartre was ill, towards the end of his life, he was almost blind and could no more write or read. She used to read to him. Of course it's terrible for anybody to be blind, but for a writer it was traumatic because he couldn't work without seeing his own writing, couldn't dictate to his secretary, he couldn't work at all. It was a terrible period. She was desperate about him, and very tired, very sad. I think those last ten years of Sartre's life killed her. She had strong health all her life, but those last years, the fear for Sartre's life . . . they destroyed her. That was why she could not support the illness she had in 1986, because she was weakened, not visibly, but deeply weakened by those terrible ten years, which she wrote about in *La Cérémonie des Adieux*. It lasted ten years. In the end she was drinking a little too much, taking too many pills, because of the constant tension, you know.

When he died it was tragic, of course, but she decided, 'I want to live,' and when she said something like that, she meant it. She recovered about two or three years afterwards, and in those last years everybody said how well she looked. Her death was almost like an accident. She wasn't ill, not at all. She had been a little sick, and went into hospital for an examination. I wasn't very anxious. We were about to go away to Biarritz for our holidays, and both of us weren't worried; but they decided it was better to do a little operation, and in fact I'm sure this operation was useless. But she could not support the shock of the anaesthetic and it was very quick; in three weeks she recovered, she was bad and she recovered, she was bad again and finally – it was so unexpected, you know. She said while she was in hospital, 'Oh, the holidays! The holidays! You haven't been away,' and I said, 'It doesn't matter, Castor, we will go in June.' It was then April. 'It doesn't matter.'

I don't remember the funeral very well, but I know there were a lot of people from all over the world and now, I'm told, there are always fresh flowers on her grave, but I never go there. There are flowers and little notes, 'Simone, we will never forget you.' Yes, there were feminists from all over the world at the graveside. It was the last *manifestation* of 1968, we said, it was the same atmosphere.

The feminist movement was very important to her. She was very concerned. She was in solidarity with all feminists, French and also foreigners, and she did everything she could for the movement. She gave a lot of interviews about feminist questions and she supported the French feminist review, *Questions Feministes*. She supported the Ministry of Rights for Women, she became a friend of Yvette Roudy and her staff and she wrote articles for her own review, *Les Temps Modernes*. But she didn't agree with those who wanted to separate men and women, the radical feminists. 'With that,' she always said, 'I don't agree. I understand why they choose this position, but I don't agree. For me, women and men must not be enemies.' And I do share these ideas.

Sartre always said he was a feminist and he *wanted* to be a feminist. He had goodwill, but he knew himself, he recognized he had bad habits with women. He was old-fashioned, treating them like children. But when she wrote *The Second Sex* he always encouraged her. He was a feminist in his thoughts, but he was

not feminist in his practice – like most, no, not most, like a lot
of men.

Only recently I came across a whole collection of letters that
Simone de Beauvoir wrote to Sartre. The letters from Sartre to
her have been published, and in them he always speaks of her
letters in reply: 'Your letters are so amusing,' and so on.
Everybody, including myself, used to ask her, 'But Castor,
where are your letters? We want to see them, too,' and she
always said she believed they had been lost during the war, or
afterwards when she moved from one hotel to another. She was
convinced her letters were lost, so I was convinced too, of course.
But suddenly just two years ago, I remember I came from my
Lycée and I was feeling bad, I came here, to her own apartment.
I was looking for some papers and in the depths of a cupboard
here I found her letters with the envelopes, so I have all the dates
and details, all the letters in reply to Sartre's. When I saw her
handwriting I understood at once what they were, it was a
marvellous moment.

I want to get them published and I've been working on
them for two years now – it's taking me a long time because her
handwriting is so awfully bad. Sartre complains about it in his
letters, 'Oh, Castor, why do you write so badly, I can't read it.'
It's true, it is awful, I have to translate it like a foreign language.

When I opened them for the first time, I felt as if I had
discovered a treasure which I was the very first person to see.
You can hear her voice in these letters. When they are published
I think she will be better understood and become closer and
more alive to people. Too often the public see her as an austere,
philosophical person, very stiff, you know, but she wasn't at all
like that. In these letters we can see her daily life, and it's very
amusing and surprising.

When she wrote her autobiography, she could not write
about everything. She said, 'I don't lie, but I can't say
everything because it involves other people.' It's not the same for
me now, because the people she wanted to protect, her friend
Olga for instance, are dead now, so I can say everything. I can
fill in the gaps.

Chronology

1908 Simone de Beauvoir born on 9 January at her parents' home, 103 Boulevard du Montparnasse, Paris.

1910 Birth of her sister, Hélène (nicknamed Poupette).

1913 Simone begins her schooling at the Cours Désir, a Catholic girls' school, at 39 rue Jacob, Montparnasse. Here, at the age of ten, she meets her beloved friend Elisabeth L., 'Zaza' in the memoirs.

1919 Due to a downturn in the family's finances, they are forced to move to a smaller flat at 71 rue de Rennes.

1924–6 Completes *baccalauréat* in philosophy and mathematics.

1927 Simone receives *certificat* in general philosophy: she is among the top three students, along with Simone Weil and Maurice Merleau-Ponty.

1929 Simone meets Sartre at the École Normale Supérieure. Several months after their first meeting they become lovers, and start to work together.
To Simone's profound distress, her friend Zaza dies at the age of twenty-one, after a tragically failed love affair with Maurice Merleau-Ponty.
Results published for the *agrégation*: at his second attempt at the examination, Sartre comes first; Simone, the youngest-ever student to pass, comes second.

1931 Simone is appointed to a full-time teaching post in Marseilles; Sartre goes to Le Havre to take up a teaching post there.

1932 Simone takes up a new teaching post in Rouen.

1933 Sartre and Simone begin their liaison with Olga Kosakievicz.

1936 Simone starts a new job teaching at the Lycée Molière in Paris, and moves to the Hôtel Royal-Bretagne, rue de la Gaité, the first of several hotels in which she is to make her home.

1937 Begins work on *L'Invitée (She Came to Stay)*, based on the triangular relationship between her, Olga and Sartre.

1939 The Second World War is declared; Sartre is drafted into the army. Simone begins to keep a journal, which is later included in *Force of Circumstance*.

1940 German occupation of Paris begins. Simone leaves Paris but soon returns. Sartre taken prisoner of war.

1941 Sartre released. The Resistance group Socialisme et Liberté is formed; Sartre and Simone join. Simone's father dies.

1943 *L'Invitée* is published.

1944 Liberation of Paris.

1945 *Le sang des autres (The Blood of Others)* is published. The magazine *Les Temps Modernes* is started. Simone is one of the founding editors.

1947 Simone goes to the United States and meets Nelson Algren; they become lovers.
She starts work on *The Second Sex*.

1949 *Le deuxième sexe (The Second Sex)* is published in two volumes, to a huge outcry from critics and French conservative society, but Simone receives many grateful letters from women readers.
Nelson Algren visits Paris.

1950 The relationship with Algren finishes.

1952 Simone starts living with Claude Lanzmann, a man many years her junior.

1953 English translation of *The Second Sex* appears in the USA and the UK.

1954 *Les Mandarins (The Mandarins)* is published, dedicated to Nelson Algren. She is awarded the prestigious Prix Goncourt.

1955   Simone buys the Paris studio apartment in which she is to live for the rest of her life, in the rue Schoelcher, with the proceeds from the Prix Goncourt. After visiting China and Moscow with Sartre, Simone settles in her new flat with Claude Lanzmann.

1958   *Memoirs d'une jeune fille rangée (Memoirs of a Dutiful Daughter)* is published and very well received. Lanzmann ceases living with Simone; they remain friends.
Simone starts her involvement in the politics of the Algerian War.
Sartre begins his chronic illness and gradual loss of sight.

1960   Albert Camus, one of Simone's oldest friends, dies.
Simone goes to Cuba with Sartre and meets Fidel Castro. Starts campaigning on behalf of Djamila Boupacha, an Algerian woman tortured by the French.
La Force de l'âge (The Prime of Life) is published, the second volume of her autobiography, and is another success.

1961   Marches with Sartre and Lanzmann for peace in Algeria, despite bomb threats to her apartment from Organization de l'Armée Secrète sympathizers. Sartre's flat is bombed because of his involvement in opposing French colonialism in Algeria.

1962   Sartre's flat is bombed again. Sartre and Simone move to a temporary flat; meanwhile more bomb threats are made to her apartment. Agreement signed to end Algerian War in March.

1963   Simone's mother dies. She starts to write *Une mort très douce (A Very Easy Death)*.
La Force des choses (Force of Circumstance) is published, the third volume of her autobiography. Begins friendship with Sylvie le Bon.

1966   *Les Belles images* published.

1968   *La Femme rompue (The Woman Destroyed)* is published.
Les événements in May – Simone and Sartre take part in many demonstrations with the students.

1970   *La vieillesse (Old Age)* is published, provoking much heated discussion in France and abroad.

Simone marches in Paris for abortion and contraception rights for women.

1971 Signs manifesto of 343 women, published in *Le Monde*, declaring they had all had an illegal abortion.
Sartre's health starts seriously deteriorating; his eyesight fails.

1972 *Tout compte fait (All Said and Done)*, the final volume of her autobiography, is published, dedicated to Sylvie le Bon.
Simone starts to fight for 'specifically feminine claims, parallel to the class struggle', and declares herself a feminist.

1974 Simone becomes President of the French League of Women's Rights.

1979 Simone's first collection of short stories is published, *Quand prime le spirituel (When Things of The Spirit come First)*, which had been rejected when she offered them for publication in 1937.

1980 Sartre dies on 15 April.

1981 *La cérémone des adieux (Adieux: A Farewell to Sartre)* is published.
Nelson Algren dies.

1983 Sartre's *Lettres au Castor et à quelques autres* is published, Simone's collection of Sartre's letters to her, edited by herself.

1986 Simone de Beauvoir dies on 14 April. Her funeral takes place at Montparnasse cemetery on 19 April, six years to the day after Sartre's funeral. Five thousand people attend.

Selected Bibliography

This list of Simone de Beauvoir's principal works gives the title and date of the original edition followed by the date in brackets of the first English translation, then the most accessible English edition is given.

L'Invitée, 1943, Gallimard, Paris. *She Came to Stay* (1949). Fontana/Flamingo, London, 1984.

Le Sang des autres, 1945, Gallimard Paris. *The Blood of Others* (1948). Penguin, Harmondsworth, 1984.

Pour une morale de l'ambiguité, 1947, Gallimard, Paris. *The Ethics of Ambiguity*, Philosophical Library, New York, 1948.

Le Deuxième sexe, vol. I 'Les faits et les mythes', vol. II 'L'expérience vécue', 1949, Paris, Gallimard. *The Second Sex*, vols. I and II (1953). Penguin, Harmondsworth, 1972; Pan/Picador, London, 1988.

Les Mandarins, 1954, Gallimard, Paris. *The Mandarins* (1957). Fontana/Flamingo, London, 1984.

La Longue marche, 1957, Gallimard, Paris. *The Long March*, André Deutsch/Weidenfeld & Nicolson, London, 1958.

Mémoirs d'une jeune fille rangée, 1958, Gallimard, Paris. *Memoirs of a Dutiful Daughter* (1959). Penguin, Harmondsworth, 1963.

La Force de l'âge, 1960, Gallimard, Paris. *The Prime of Life* (1962). Penguin, Harmondsworth, 1968.

La Force des choses, 1963, Gallimard, Paris. *Force of Circumstance* (1965). Penguin, Harmondsworth, 1968.

Une mort très douce, 1964, Gallimard, Paris. *A Very Easy Death* (1966). Penguin, Harmondsworth, 1969.

Les belles images, 1966, Gallimard, Paris. *Les Belles Images* (1968). Fontana/Flamingo, London, 1984.

La Femme rompue, 1968, Gallimard, Paris. *The Woman Destroyed* (1969). Fontana/Flamingo, London, 1984.

La Vieillesse, 1970, Gallimard, Paris. *Old Age* (1972). Penguin, Harmondsworth, 1977.

Tout compte fait, 1972, Gallimard, Paris. *All Said and Done* (1974). Penguin, Harmondsworth, 1977.

Quand prime le spirituel, 1979, Gallimard, Paris. *When Things of the Spirit Come First* (1982). Fontana/Flamingo, London, 1983.

La Cérémonie des adieux, suivi des entretiens avec Jean-Paul Sartre, 1981, Gallimard, Paris. *Adieux: A Farewell to Sartre* (1984). Penguin, Harmondsworth, 1985.

Lettres au Castor et à quelques autres by Jean-Paul Sartre, edited by Simone de Beauvoir, 1983, Gallimard, Paris.

The following are the most recent biographies of Simone de Beauvoir, which also give references for many other appraisals of her life and work:

Simone de Beauvoir, Lisa Appignanesi, Penguin Books, Harmondsworth, 1988.

Simone de Beauvoir: A Feminist Mandarin, Mary Evans, Tavistock, London, 1985.

Simone de Beauvoir, Claude Francis and Fernande Gontier, Sidgwick & Jackson, London, 1987.

Simone de Beauvoir: A Re-Reading, Judith Okely, Virago Press, London, 1986.

Simone de Beauvoir Today, Alice Schwartzer, Chatto & Windus/Hogarth Press, London, 1984.

Two recent biographies of Jean-Paul Sartre – *Sartre*, Annie Cohen-Salal, Gallimard, Paris 1985; and *Writing Against*, Ronald Hayman, Weidenfeld & Nicolson, London, 1986, present a different perspective from that of de Beauvoir's volumes of autobiography.